APPLIED RESEARCH +DESIGN PUBLISHING

Published by Applied Research and Design Publishing, an imprint of ORO Editions.
Gordon Goff: Publisher

www.appliedresearchanddesign.com
info@appliedresearchanddesign.com

USA, EUROPE, ASIA, MIDDLE EAST, SOUTH AMERICA

Author: Plan:b Architects
Text: Felipe Mesa
Foreword: Andrés Jaque
Comments: Emilio Tuñón – Federico Soriano
Book Design: Mesa Estándar / Juan David Díez – Miguel Mesa
Project Coordinator: Alejandro Guzman-Avila
Managing Editor: Jake Anderson

Images:
Alejandro Arango: Pages 14,17, 21, 23, 24, 27, 28, 30, 32, 33, 41, 42, 43, 46, 49, 51, 54, 57, 58, 59, 65, 67 up, 70, 73, 75, 78, 83 up, 89, 90, 94, 97 up, 98, 99, 102, 105, 106, 107, 110, 113, 114, 115, 118.
Cristóbal Palma: Pages 129, 134, 135.
Iwan Baan: Pages 35, 37, 121, 122, 126, 130.
Julián Castro: Pages 67 down, 81, 83 down, 86.
Sergio Gómez: Pages 18, 57, 58, 59, 62, 97 down.

10 9 8 7 6 5 4 3 2 1 First Edition

Library of Congress data available upon request. World Rights: Available

ISBN: 978-1-951541-42-2

Color Separations and Printing:
ORO Group Ltd.
Printed in China.

International Distribution: www.appliedresearchanddesign.com/distribution

ORO Editions makes a continuous effort to minimize the overall carbon footprint of its publications. As part of this goal, ORO Editions, in association with Global ReLeaf, arranges to plant trees to replace those used in the manufacturing of the paper produced for its books. Global ReLeaf is an international campaign run by American Forests, one of the world's oldest nonprofit conservation organizations. Global ReLeaf is American Forests' education and action program that helps individuals, organizations, agencies, and corporations improve the local and global environment by planting and caring for trees.

PLAN: B ARCHITECTS
12 PROJECTS
IN 120 CONSTRAINTS

TEXT: FELIPE MESA

CONTENTS

FOREWORD

```
F    W    F W    F    W    F W    F    W    F W    F    W
O    O    O O    O    O    O O    O    O    O O    O    O
R    R    R R    R    O    R R    R    R    R R    R    R
E    D    E D    E    D    E D    E    D    E D    E    D
·    ·    · ·    ·    ·    · ·    ·    ·    · ·    ·    ·
F    W    F W    F    W    F W    F    W    F W    F    W
O    O    O O    O    O    O O    O    O    O O    O    O
R    R    R R    R    R    R R    R    R    R R    R    R
E    D    E D    E    D    E D    E    D    E D    E    D
·    ·    · ·    ·    ·    · ·    ·    ·    · ·    ·    ·
F    W    F W    F    W    F W    F    W    F W    F    W
O    O    O O    O    O    O O    O    O    O O    O    O
R    R    R R    R    R    R R    R    R    R R    R    R
E    D    E D    E    D    E D    E    D    E D    E    D
·    ·    · ·    ·    ·    · ·    ·    ·    · ·    ·    ·
F    W    F W    F    W    F W    F    W    F W    F    W
O    O    O O    O    O    O O    O    O    O O    O    O
R    R    R R    R    R    R R    R    R    R R    R    R
E    D    E D    E    D    E D    E    D    E D    E    D
·    ·    · ·    ·    ·    · ·    ·    ·    · ·    ·    ·
F    W    F W    F    W    F W    F    W    F W    F    W
O    O    O O    O    O    O O    O    O    O O    O    O
R    R    R R    R    R    R R    R    R    R R    R    R
E    D    E D    E    D    E D    E    D    E D    E    D
·    ·    · ·    ·    ·    · ·    ·    ·    · ·    ·    ·
F    W    F W    F    W    F W    F    W    F W    F    W
O    O    O O    O    O    O O    O    O    O O    O    O
R    R    R R    R    R    R R    R    R    R R    R    R
E    D    E D    E    D    E D    E    D    E D    E    D
·    ·    · ·    ·    ·    · ·    ·    ·    · ·    ·    ·
F    W    F W    F    W    F W    F    W    F W    F    W
O    O    O O    O    O    O O    O    O    O O    O    O
R    R    R R    R    R    R R    R    R    R R    R    R
E    D    E D    E    D    E D    E    D    E D    E    D
·    ·    · ·    ·    ·    · ·    ·    ·    · ·    ·    ·
F    W    F W    F    W    F W    F    W    F W    F    W
O    O    O O    O    O    O O    O    O    O O    O    O
R    R    R R    R    R    R R    R    R    R R    R    R
E    D    E D    E    D    E D    E    D    E D    E    D
·    ·    · ·    ·    ·    · ·    ·    ·    · ·    ·    ·
F    W    F W    F    W    F W    F    W    F W    F    W
O    O    O O    O    O    O O    O    O    O O    O    O
R    R    R R    R    R    R R    R    R    R R    R    R
E    D    E D    E    D    E D    E    D    E D    E    D
·    ·    · ·    ·    ·    · ·    ·    ·    · ·    ·    ·
F    W    F W    F    W    F W    F    W    F W    F    W
O    O    O O    O    O    O O    O    O    O O    O    O
R    R    R R    R    R    R R    R    R    R R    R    R
E    D    E D    E    D    E D    E    D    E D    E    D
·    ·    · ·    ·    ·    · ·    ·    ·    · ·    ·    ·
```

If something marks the times we live in, it is the need to multiply the spectrum of possibility by sensing the limits of the contexts which we live by. We expand, mix, and love because we, vulnerable beings, know how much we depend on others. This is what fuels Felipe and Federico Mesa along with the momentous contribution to today's architecture through the work of their office, Plan: b. Projects such as the Embera School, the San Vicente Community Center, and the Santo Domingo Kindergarten carefully came to existence as entangled within the life of people, animals, air, soil, economies, and the conflicts of those who are transformed by them. As Felipe Mesa explains in *ANGLES* (included in this book), entanglement is not a painful way to adapt to what already exists, nor is it an intellectual self-imposed *divertiment*. Identifying limits is the gentle move to enact construction not as a way for humans to exploit others — other people, other environments, others within ourselves — but rather foster the conditions that allow inclusive forms of collective co-emergency to happen.

In 2006 shortly after graduating as an architect, Felipe Mesa created Orquideorama with Alejandro Bernal, Camilo and J. Paul Restrepo. The Orquideorama became part of a movement for human-centered activism, intended to redistribute the power of architecture to those historically disposed of it. All thought went to the social space the canopy created. But the orchids never really found their way into the story. When I met Felipe at that time, he kept insisting on the extraordinary beauty of these presences — that he would explain as constituted in watery air. Fifteen years later, in light of Plan: b's later work, the social element of Orquideorama's social space was not one to be occupied by zipped-up self-contained humans, but instead that of the watery, airy commons, of muddy geologies, and the magnetized atmospheres where orchids, with others, gain bodied solidarity.

Plan: b's architecture expands horizontally, attached to the earthy and to the aqueous. Could they possibly speak of any of the buildings included in this book without explaining the soils, rocks, and swamps they are muddled in? Jardin School is built on top of a fault. It is constructed on the footprint of two now-gone educational buildings. This architecture does not need its ground to be "new." It finds its role in reconnecting troubled remains that are out of the architects' control. The Mesa brothers and their team don't serve humans, nor do they indulge themselves in claiming that they make humans "better"; rather, they make breathing, sweating, peeing, bleeding, and decomposing sites of togetherness.

MUD AND ORCHIDS. PLAN: B'S BODIED SOLIDARITY

Andrés Jaque

INTRODUCTION

Our creative work in architecture has been carried out for the last twenty years in the Colombian context and mainly in Antioquia and the city of Medellin. Colombia is a tropical country, with a wide variety of ecosystems (tropical rain forests, high altitude grass-lands, coastal vegetation, deserts) and human populations (European, Native Amerindian, Afro-descendant, Mestizos). Although it has a democracy of more than one hundred and eighty years, its stability has been intermittently affected — especially since the second half of the 20th century, due to countryside violence and the rise of drug trafficking. In the global economic context, even if Colombia is a recent member of the OECD (Organization for Economic Co-operation and Development), it still has many of the characteristics of a developing country. All these particularities have configured a restricted context for the practice of a quality architecture (a situation that is not exclusive to Colombia): limited budgets and technologies, reduced cultural exchanges, limited educational environment, and social inequity.

This is the context under which we became architects, therefore, working under these conditions has been natural and inevitable. It has led us to understand architecture as a positive expression of the various types of constraints that configure it (implicit and explicit forces). In our projects, we usually avoid what is not necessary and take advantage of available technologies and materials; we dodge complex geometries that usually increase budgets, and we strive to build clear arguments to support the minimal choices we make. Accepting restrictions as the primary material of architecture often implies some creative advantages (the field of action narrows, options reduce, and situations are left to decide for you), and brings design closer to everyday realities. Under these circumstances, we aim to make our architecture flexible, available, and permeable to these ever-present constraints[1]. The idea of complexity that is useful in this case is not only related to the form or program of the project but to the whole process inherent in the design, construction, and future performance of the building. For us, constraints imply complexity, and complexity leads us to quality architecture.

We understand creativity in architecture as an activity almost entirely determined by the context and its constraints. Although this seems obvious, it is far from typical explanations and arguments that professional architects and students make about their work. By typical, we mean the conventional and widespread ideas about how creativity takes place, which implies isolated, emotional labor, an abstracted singularity, and disconnection from everyday realities. Some dose of this reflective work can indeed be stimulating. Still, from our point of view, when designing an architecture project, the most challenging issue is the construction of agreements that allow us to fit in a qualified way in the specific constraints of each project. Unconsciously architects do it, and this does not entail that personal ways of understanding disciplinary problems disappear. For us, the form does not follow function, or climate, but rather a conglomerate of the changing constraints of each project. Not only is the form an expression of the prevalent restrictions; so are the programs, techniques, uses, and even the geometry.

A constraint is something that limits one's freedom of action or choice. It is "the state of being checked, restricted, or compelled to avoid or perform some action."[2] We can understand the constraints in architecture as opportunities to propose more precise and focused strategies, or solutions. As paradoxical as it may seem, clear restrictions enable increased robust and more direct design solutions, by emphasizing what is essential and placing in the background the whims or inexplicable obsessions of the authors. Constraints also propitiate the establishment of solid supporting arguments to all decisions involved in the design of a project, while making emphasis on collaboration and shared knowledge.

In our projects, a wide range of unavoidable constraints are present, with varying influences according to the particular conditions of each commission: the soil features, the ecological impacts, the material cycles, the availability of public services, available technologies, labor, cultural behaviors, economic realities, urban or safety regulations, wishes or requests of the affected communities, etc. We think that understanding these restrictions as the most relevant material of the project, the design strategy is open to the various actors and forces involved, and becomes more participatory and less imposed.

How many independent decisions can an architect make when designing a building? And how many are due to the negotiation processes inherent to each project? In our case, the answer is simple: we make a few decisions, but in our process, we drive forces, offer varied options, open alternatives, and soften impositions; we build agreements[3].

In this book, we review a set of Plan: b projects in Colombia through the environmental, social, and voluntary constraints we faced, and the interim agreements we built around them. We will carry out a reconstruction of the central facts behind these buildings through an "inverse" exercise — explaining each project based on contextual constraints and not on singular architectural ideas. But before that, and to approach this matter from various angles, we will briefly review and comment on theoretical proposals, notions, and points of view of authors that are related to the idea of creative work under constraints: Michael Baxandall (art historian), Jon Elster (social and political theorist), Enrique Walker (architect), Stan Allen (architect), Carles Muro (architect), David Byrne (musician), Jorgen Leth, Lars von Trier and Thomas Vinterberg (film directors), and Bob Gill (graphic designer); as an exemption to the rule, we will mention the ideas of an author in opposition to this tradition — Philip Johnson (architect) — and finally we will briefly explain the Chinese Tangram, a paradigmatic game that arises from simple restrictions, expressed in a great diversity of two-dimensional geometric figures. By reviewing the work of other authors and the way they understand the limitations and difficulties that are part of their creative activity, we attempt to generate a broad reflective base to approach our architectural projects and the predominant role that restrictions have played in them.

THREE QUESTIONS. THREE TYPES OF CONSTRAINTS. OBS... ... THREE MET... NCEPT. SEV... S. ONE... VE OBS... NE VOW OF CHASTITY PROBLEMS. SEVEN FIGURES

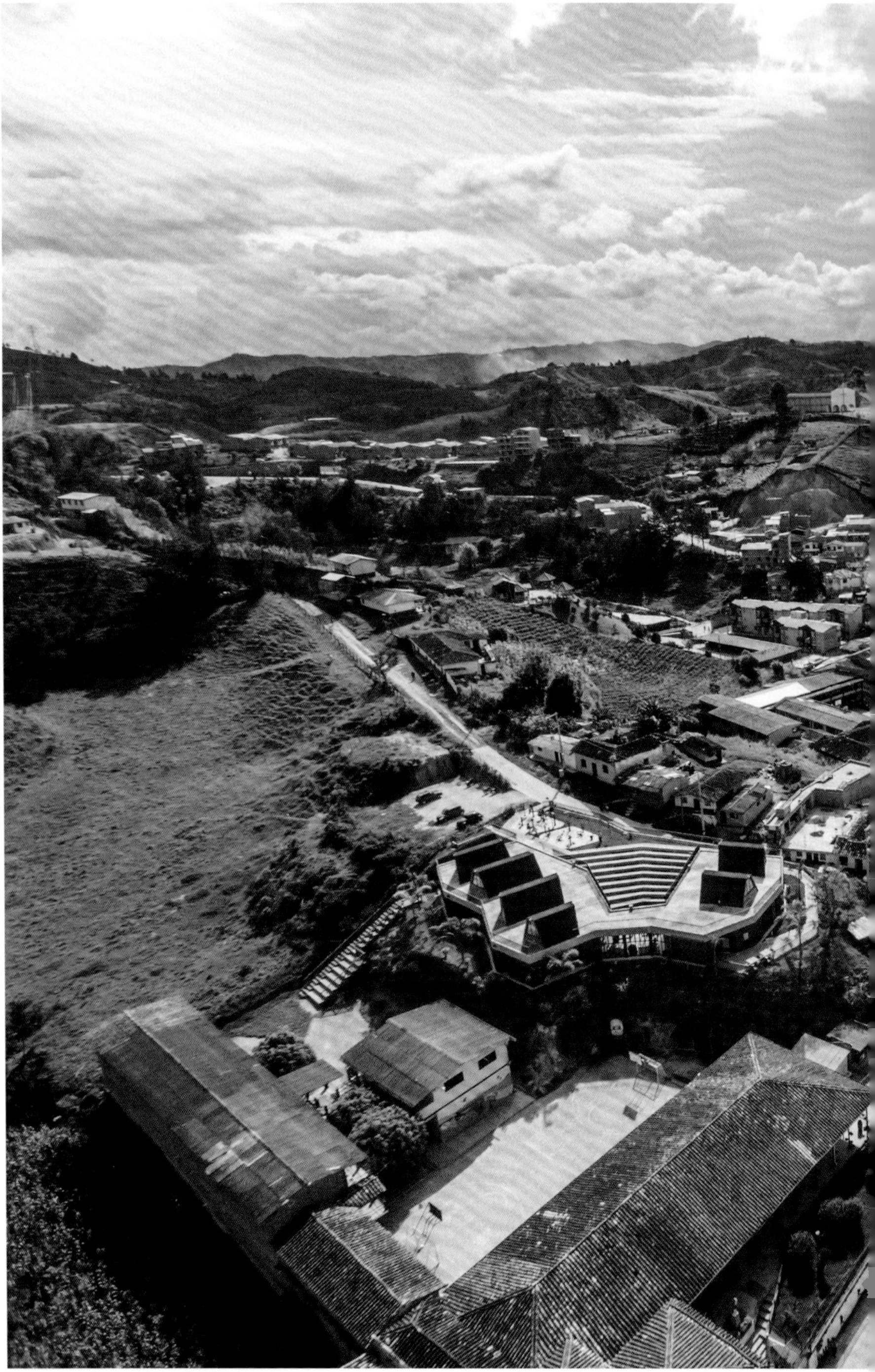

In his 1985 book *Patterns of Intentions*[1], the British art historian and professor Michael Baxandall, proposes a method for studying historical objects — taking as an example the Forth Bridge in Scotland (designed by Benjamin Baker, completed in 1889). For Baxandall, the explanation of a building lies in answering three questions: why it exists, why it is so, what is the specific culture that makes it possible. The first question refers to the charge — if something exists, it is because someone ordered it and was willing to pay for it — in which there are explicit requests and various constraints. A type of cause to the building's form follows from the commission, but according to Baxandall, these are usually not the leading causes to justify it. For Baxandall, question two ("why is it so") is the crucial one. The building is built as it is because someone, the architect, made a series of decisions. They have their tastes, preferences, way of doing things, interests, and they might even have been self-restraining. If the commission is what we usually consider "the problem," the author's work is "the solution." The author brings to this intellectual operation (commission-solution) methods that come from his trajectory and that, according to Baxandall, substantially coloring the formal result. Although the third question is not asked explicitly in Baxandall's text, it is implicitly and connected with the previous two. Question three refers to what is considered exemplary in each period — the taste or spirit of the moment, the material and spiritual circumstances that surround the project, and the availability of materials or technologies at hand. Here, we can identify constraints and causes linked to the specific culture.

We intrepret our San Vicente Ferrer Community Center in Antioquia as the convergence of spatial preferences of the community, the availability of traditional materials, and the topographic characteristics of the terrain. In some community workshops, the local people repeatedly drew a building with a central courtyard or an outdoor theater. They requested the use of local materials such as rustic brown stone and cement tiles, and suggested visual contact with the existing church. The available lot, an irregular fragment of a mountain, determined the building's position — which we designed following the geometry of the topographic lines. The soil technical aspects and the requests of the client and the community were decisive in the design. Our choices were subtle. Although in this text, we as architects, explain some of our buildings (they are not historical objects), Baxandall's method is relevant because he understands the project as a convergence of various circumstances instead of an individual and free expression of the author. The building is a solution to the problem under specific conditions. What is crucial is not the architect's preferences, but their ability to manage the various constraints to place them at the service of the project's qualities.

THREE QUESTIONS

THREE TYPES OF CONSTRAINTS

"Constraints and Conventions in the Arts" is the third chapter of the 2000 book *Ulysses Unbound*[2], in which the Norwegian social and political theorist Jon Elster, proposes three types of constraints that any artist or architect normally faces: intrinsic constraints, that are given and are, for example, inherent to the structural limitations of the material; imposed constraints, that come from external agents — persons or institutions commissioning a building — such as budgets, municipal regulations, aesthetic preferences of a client, etc; self-imposed constraints, which come from the author himself and normally seek to strengthen his work. For Elster, "the restrictions imposed on or chosen by the artist can take many forms. A basic distinction is between hard constraints and soft constraints or conventions. Hard constraints are formal, material, technical, or financial restrictions on the selection and combination of the constituent units of the given medium. Conventions, as the word indicates, are restrictions that constitute a specific genre such as the sonnet or the classical symphony." We see conventions in architecture as formats, typologies, programs, and styles. For Elster, intrinsic, imposed and self-imposed constraints are different in creative terms: "On the one hand, preexisting or preset constraints enhance and stimulate the creative process. On the other hand, the creation of constraints is itself part of that process."

In our design for the Puerto Triunfo Community Center in Antioquia, we faced various intrinsic and imposed constraints. Our client and his advisors requested a resistant, low-maintenance construction that would take as reference some tropical buildings made of reinforced concrete. The budgetary limitations did not allow air conditioning, and the warm and humid climate of the place forced us to propose a permeable building affected by the municipal regulations of a corner lot. Our visit to a nearby ruin, in which concrete block walls configured shaded spaces amid native gardens, led us to work with some simple self-imposed constraints: using reinforced concrete as the primary building material (structure, facade, floor); to locate the structure on the perimeter to generate flexible interior spaces; to design a deep facade allowing the growth of gardens. From our perspective, intrinsic, imposed, and self-imposed constraints have changing influences according to the particularities of each project. We believe that under substantial imposed restrictions there is still room for quality architecture; although there is not much to decide, it is still crucial to guide contextual forces properly.

The Chilean architect Enrique Walker wrote the article titled "Scaffoldings" for the 2012 book *From Rules to Constraints*[3], a publication about the professional and academic work of Spanish architects Luis M. Mansilla and Emilio Tuñon. In this text, Walker diversely understands work under constraints, which moves between recurring and novel results: "The meeting of constraints is by definition a chance encounter. Sometimes their meeting is tight and may prevent any action. Sometimes, their meeting is loose and may allow for any action. Sometimes, their meeting is predictable and may lead to recurrent solutions. Sometimes their meeting is unexpected and may potentially lead to invention." In his viewpoint, architects would dismiss constraints as obstacles to the imagination and accept them as requirements to meet. Only in a few exceptions, architects see limitations as the possibility of finding unexpected design problems. For Walker, some architects move from concept to constraints, and others move from constraints to the concept. From their point of view, voluntary restraints can incite unexpected encounters with imposed limitations and thus redirect problems; voluntary restrictions are arbitrary when facing the initial problem but not towards its redefinition.

OBSTACLES

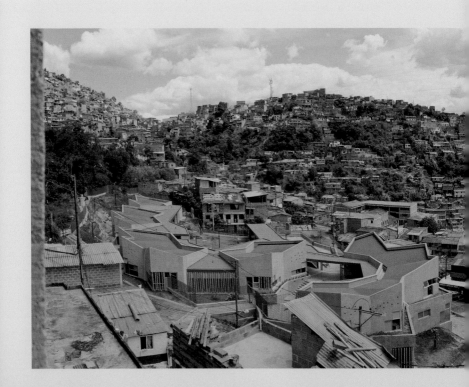

When we designed the Santo Domingo Kindergarten in Medellin, some constraints became arguments to develop the project. The impossibility of using dynamite to remove large rocks inside the terrain led us to propose a stepped building that adapts to the existing topography without the need of massive earthworks. The irregular shape of the lot led us to use a modular geometry, easily adaptable. The use of light colors (blue and green) defined by the client, allowed the building to connect with the local, diverse, and colorful architecture. Our choice of using only pentagonal modules allowed us to create a unique and angular building, easily recognizable in the neighborhood. As we can see, constraints are phenomena deeply linked to specific and concrete realities of the project. Because of that, they limit options, clarify possibilities, and reveal what is feasible and even unexpected. In our design process, we try to articulate constraints and arguments simultaneously: constraints detonate arguments, and arguments are embedded in restrictions.

In his 2017 book *Four Projects*[4], the American architect Stan Allen published a conversation he had in 2016 with Enrique Walker about architectural design under rules and constraints (referring to the Luis M. Mansilla and Emilio Tuñon book *From Rules to Constraints*). For Allen, this approach to design, and specifically in his practice, could be defined as algorithmic (from a broad perspective): "a set of rules for solving a problem in a finite number of steps." For him, even if every project deserves to be addressed on its terms and their rules emerge in response to specific constraints, old ideas could come back in response to particular problems, without arbitrarily forcing the rules. Allen also proposes a distinction between restrictions imposed by a specific issue or architect (site, program, geometry) and constraints that are part of a shared disciplinary legacy (patterns of thought and ways of working). That last idea imposes another constraint: "You have to speak in a language that is intelligible to the discipline as a whole."

RULES

To design the Embera School in Vigía del Fuerte (for a Colombian native community), we defined a group of simple rules based on various restrictions: use traditional geometries and volumes, close to local constructions; avoid the use of native wood in the risk of extinction; use reinforced concrete for the elevated base of the building, and light metal material for the rest of the structure; locate the program at the long ends to create a covered street; connect the building with the existing elevated sidewalks. It is possible to address some constraints through general and constant rules, but in most cases, restrictions are linked to specific circumstances that require particular strategies, materials, and geometries.

22

More than a few contemporary architects (e.g. Carles Muro, Enrique
Walker, Stan Allen, Emilio Tuñon, Luis M. Mansilla to name a few)
have been interested in the work of the Oulipo Group (Workshop
for Potential Literature). This group of writers and mathematicians,
founded in 1960 by Raymond Queneau and Francois Le
Lionnais, included the participation of notable figures
such as George Perec and Italo Calvino. In *The Penguin
Book of Oulipo*[5], editor and writer Philip Terry defines
the aim of this group as the exploration of the benefits of
mathematics and rule-based constraints for the writing of
literature. For him, "Hidden behind the word 'constraint'
three principal methods stand out: (i) strict constraints,
such as writing without the letter 'e', as in Perec's novel *La
disparition* (*A Void*), or the constraints of form involved in
fixed-form poetries; (ii) what Oulipo refers to as 'combi-
natorial literature', as in Raymond Queneau's Cent mille milliards de
poèmes (*A Hundred Thousand Billion Poems*); and (iii) techniques of
transforming or 'translating' existing texts, such as their famous N+7
method, where all nouns are changed by going on seven places in a
dictionary: 'To be, or not to be, that is the quiche.'"

In our design for the Siete Vueltas School in San Juan de Urabá, we
decided to group small modular buildings around an existing soccer
field that had to be kept. We used the same structural system and materials in all buildings to solve strict transport and budget constraints.
By connecting the buildings through a covered corridor, we defined a
large permeable "ring" adapted to the hot and dry climate of the place.
In architecture, working under constraints is not optional, especially
in terms of external limitations, and that is why we usually define the
possibilities of each project through a network of imposed constraints
— adding some nuances through voluntary restrictions. In our case,
self-imposed limitations are not typically arbitrary, and we try to move
away from too abstract compositional exercises because they usually
seem artificial and unnecessary.

In his 2002 article "Hacia una Arquitectura Potencial" ("Towards a Potential Architecture") published in the #97 Circo magazine[6], the Catalan architect Carles Muro reviews examples in which some architects decide relevant aspects of their projects based on various constraints such as materials, transportation, and municipal regulations. In 1928 Mies van der Rohe defined the height of the German pavilion in Barcelona (310 cm) according to the size of an appropriate Onyx block found in Hamburg. James Stirling designed the pavilion for Electa at the Venice Biennale (1991) using a construction system determined by the available boat transportation. Kazuo Shinohara defined the overall geometry of a house in Tokyo (1981) using the mandatory withdrawals from nearby high-voltage lines. Through their examples, Muro shows how external forces restrict but do not entirely define some formal solutions, and he states his interest in projects configured through positive external limitations that incorporate new self-imposed and specific constraints. He proposes the concept of "potential architecture," alluding to the work of the Oulipo group in the field of literature and its production based on the use of formal, structural, and to some extent, arbitrary restrictions.

When we designed the Jardin School in Antioquia, the main external force that restricted the project was the low resistance of the ground. We defined the elongated and narrow position of the buildings according to the strips of stable terrain. Under this situation, we proposed a concave construction, shaping a large patio, and a convex construction, forming a terrace open to the landscape. Employing these new low and elongated buildings, we consolidated two white marks visible in the distance, in the middle of the landscape of coffee crops and native forests. In this way, the educational program stands out unexpectedly in the middle of the rural context. Responding to the problematic characteristics of the terrain that conditioned the weight, height, and shape of the buildings, we designed a project in close relationship with the rural landscape, without initially being our intention. Some restrictions have the potential to trigger positive and unexpected phenomena.

ONE CONCEPT

The Seven Crutches of Modern Architecture (remarks from an informal talk to students of architecture at Harvard)[7] is a 1955 text written by the American architect Philip Johnson, evidence in a fun way a rejection of constraints as positive obstacles or creative tools. For him, the true architecture is something that is beyond the seven crutches he proposes in the text: history, pretty drawings, utility, comfort, cheapness, serving the client, and structure. Still, in reality, these crutches are nothing more than a useful compendium of constraints inherent to architecture and its context (cultural, disciplinary, technical, economic, social, and ethical constraints). For Johnson, the architecture project is not the qualified convergence of the seven crutches, but an act of independent creation, isolated and without rules. Architecture is the sum of "artistic" and inevitable decisions that the author must make in isolation. Although he does not propose what an artistic decision is, he implies it is a compositional, formal, abstract, and autonomous activity.

SEVEN CRUTCHES

Our design for the San Vicente School in Antioquia consisted of a sum of architectural decisions made in collaboration with our client, the community, and the team of engineers. Due to budget constraints, we designed a simple concrete structure and used conventional materials. Responding to space limitations, we developed a compact two-story building, replicating the polygonal geometry of the lot. Faced with our client's preferences, we designed a closed facade with a few rectangular windows to the outside. Responding to municipal regulations, we located at the ends of the building a ramp and a staircase that helped to consolidate the enclosure. Faced with requests from the community, we kept the existing small soccer field, opening the interior facade to the distant landscape. For us, the architectural project is in itself an imperfect crutch that implies the construction of agreements and the articulation of inevitable and voluntary constraints. The project is a contextual device that can potentially help us to live better, or a provisional consolidation of contextual forces, partially directed by the author.

In his 2012 book *How Music Works*[8], the American musician David Byrne proposes that artists of various disciplines (writers, musicians, architects, sculptors, painters) unconsciously and instinctively create their works to fit into preexisting formats. For him, previous contextual restrictions guide the individual sense of emotional strength. The form that the work of any artist takes is always predetermined and opportunistic ("meaning one makes something because of the opportunity is there"), even if it is involuntary. From his point of view, we work in reverse, moving from the forces of the context towards our projects and not in the opposite direction; we work to fit in situations and available opportunities that broadly define the qualities, formats, and characteristics of our works.

ONE DIRECTION

In the design of the Hontanares School in Envigado, we followed this direction: topography - program - earthwork - users - structure - materials - landscape. According to the topographic diversity of the terrain, we defined the strategic distribution of the program, and for this, we did an accurate earthwork. We avoided building on the central plateau and favored constructions along the slopes. We made the entire school on two levels connected by ramps, allowing the fluid movement of students. We defined a reinforced concrete structure, with a cantilever roof to cover the corridors, and we chose inexpensive materials to set modular buildings connected to the rural landscape. The idea of moving in reverse (from constraints to the project) and fitting into preexisting situations describes the direction in which our architectural practice has naturally flowed. On the one hand, we are interested in an architecture connected to specific circumstances in a qualified way. On the other hand, we believe that in terms of the projects, the material received is often more important than the one proposed[9].

The Five Obstructions[10] is a 2003 Danish documentary film directed by Lars von Trier and Jörgen Leth. The first one proposes to his former professor Leth, five obstacles[11] to remake his short film *The Perfect Human*[12]. Lars von Trier's obstructions push Leth to move from constraints — intrinsic, imposed, and voluntary — to the field of his preferences as an artist, and not the other way around. Von Trier forces Leth to go from the perfection of the original short film to the complexity of everyday life expressed in the new documentary, in which there is no longer a "perfect" human or a neutral context, but different ways of being human and various active environments. They replace the original architecture background of the initial document by a group of diverse architectures determined by their specific realities. The "perfect" human inhabits an abstract and timeless space, while the "imperfect" human inhabits the temporal spaces of restricted realities and techniques.

In our design for the Click Clack Hotel in Medellin, we can list the following obstructions that were defined by our client's preferences, by technical situations or municipal regulations: the building must be built in an accelerated way, using a prefabricated metal structure; the building must comply with two municipal regulations that overlap in the lot and that allow shifting heights and overhangs; the building must offer a permeable and open space on the ground floor; the building must be designed as the stacking of habitable capsules of different sizes, giving a unitary appearance; the building must be monochromatic. Each project faces its realities through changing and successive obstructions, using a varied group of strategies. It is not only a matter of making the best of limited situations but to get in touch with these restricted circumstances, to get to know them, and to be able to propose a necessary architecture that is close to the users — that is flexible and perhaps less imposed.

In 1995, eight years before *The Five Obstructions* was filmed, Danish film directors Lars von Trier and Thomas Vinterberg wrote the "Dogma 95" manifesto and their set of rules "The Vow of Chastity." [13] Those two documents would be the base to form the Dogma 95 collective, which was later joined by Kristian Levring and Sören Kragh-Jacobsen. Behind the work of this collective, there is not only a criticism of big-budget commercial cinema, full of technological tricks and makeup, but also a criticism of auteur cinema obsessed with personal styles — in many cases isolated and hermetic. Faced with films that make artificial illusions, Dogma 95 proposes a non-individual, raw, and emotional cinema. For Thomas Vinterberg, Dogma 95 is his attempt to "undress film," or to reach the "naked film." The most recognized films of the collective are Vinterberg's *Festen* ("The Celebration")[14] and von Trier's *Idioterne* ("The Idiots")[15]. Vinterberg and von Trier designed an exhaustive set of self-imposed constraints. Although they had to make it a little flexible from the start (Vinterberg covered a window in *The Celebration*, and von Trier used background music in *The Idiots*), in reality, these restrictions allowed them to get closer to the actors, characters and the filmed context. They not only used the available technological means but tried to put their tastes in the background. We can argue that their aesthetic preference was precisely to work under restrictions that pushed them to make direct cinema avoiding the makeup. In their case, voluntary constraints serve as strict limitations.

When designing the Antejardin Office Building in Medellin, we defined our own "vow of chastity" (a title for our own voluntary restrictions) to avoid not only the construction of an abstract structure with a neutral glass facade — the typical *international* office building — but also to prevent the development of an impermeable building, with high energy consumption and without bioclimatic qualities, isolated from Medellin's tropical climate: the building must have deep and shady facades, with balconies, terraces, and gardens; the building must have operable doors and windows to allow cross-ventilation; the building must be constructed with rustic and opaque materials, incorporating different textures; the building must consolidate a curved and smooth corner that accompanies the movement of pedestrians; the building must have direct contact with the street, avoiding fences. From our point of view, the Dogma 95 proposals have echoed when one thought of some of the characteristics of much of the contemporary architecture: an obsession with technological innovation and digital representational tools, and with an autonomous and personal work, full of formal "tricks." The idea of an "undressed" cinema allows us to think about the concept of a "naked" architecture, not in the sense of reduction but, in the sense of rawness with everyday realities. In our practice and through our networks of changing constraints, we do not try to simplify our projects but approach them flexibly and directly. We face constant imposed restrictions that sharply limit the project scope (for example, avoiding the use of tricks), and perhaps that is why our voluntary constraints are usually mild. Putting our preferences in the background is also an aesthetic posture.

In his 1981 book, *Forget All the Rules You Ever Learned About Graphic Design. Including the Ones in This Book*[16], American graphic designer Bob Gill understands the exercise of his discipline as a process to solve specific communication problems and not as a compositional, isolated, and abstract activity. For Gill, graphic ideas are solutions to particular problems: they should not seem arbitrary and should give the impression of inevitability. If the problems are not attractive, the designer's task is to rethink them: qualified ideas arise from suggestive problems, and graphic strategies and their components (styles, techniques, fonts, colors, etc.) emerge naturally as an extension of ideas linked to specific problems. His process seems to function as a subtle mix of received constraints, redirected employing graphic and voluntary restrictions. When Gill proposes to forget all the learned rules, he does not mean to work with more freedom, but to ignore the rules that force you to work mechanically with preset styles to rethink problems and connect directly with their constrained realities.

PROBLEMS

When we designed the Four Sports Facilities in Medellin, the available space was small and narrow to accommodate four different constructions. Therefore, we understood the new project as a great "built continent," made up of various programs, covered streets, squares, and gardens. Through a system of roofs made up of parallel strips, we covered sports activities and public spaces, creating shade on the east-west sides and allowing cross ventilation on the north-south sides. The answer to the problem was the design of a compact and permeable building with bioclimatic qualities. We try to enable the forces involved in each project to determine or demand specific design strategies. We avoid having previous intentions, and when we do it, we must adapt them to the particular circumstances of the commission.

SEVEN FIGURES

The Tangram[17] is a Chinese puzzle that became popular in Europe in the early 19th century. The game consists of the articulation of seven flat shapes to form different figures. When we stored these seven pieces, they form a perfect square. When we combine them, they can produce more than 1,600 different configurations including animals, plants, buildings, people, letters, numbers, objects, etc. The seven shapes are two large right triangles, one medium right triangle, two small right triangles, one square, and one parallelogram. The rules are straightforward: figures cannot overlap and must move adjacently. The parallelogram is the only piece that may need to be flipped when forming certain figures, since it has rotational symmetry but no reflection symmetry. Every time we play Tangram, a simple set of intrinsic, imposed, and voluntary constraints come into play. The geometry of the seven flat shapes and their rules of movement are inherent in the game. The choice to only build figures of people, for example, can be an imposed restriction, and the voluntary effort so that all these figures are dynamic and involve an activity (walking, dancing, exercising, etc.), would work as a self-imposed constraint. With a limited group of pieces and a significant number of combinations, it is not only possible to obtain a diversity of figures, but also to endow them with specific qualities: movement, strength, delicacy, rigidity, etc. In that way, the resulting silhouettes are located in an ambiguous place between figuration and abstraction, trying to get closer to reality, but within their limitations.

In our Orquideorama project in Medellin, we used equal hexagons to form modules of seven elements. By connecting thirteen modules in various positions, the result was a changing figure, adaptable to the irregular void of the native forest. Although the final geometry is regular and abstract, it also recalls the shape of a cluster of flowers. In this building, three-dimensionality and repetition configured a porous space, which surpassed in complexity the initial two-dimensional figures. The Tangram seems like a useful metaphor to explain the architecture that we are able to design. Through simple geometries, technologies close to our reality, changing combinations, and qualities that work as slight nuances, we approach configurations that are halfway between abstraction and figuration with a dynamic will that always have implicit the constraints at stake.

SAN VICENTE COMMUNITY CENTER.PUERTO TRIUNFO

12 PROJECTS IN 120 CONSTRAINTS

San Vicente Community Center.
Puerto Triunfo Community
Center.
Santo Domingo Kindergarten.
Embera School.
Siete Vueltas School.
Jardin School.
San Vicente School.
Hontanares School.
Click Clack Hotel - Medellin.
Antejardin.
Four Sport Facilities.
Orquideorama.

COM SANTO DOM TEN. EMB :TE VUEI DIN SCHO SCHOOL. HON·IANARES SCHOOL.CLICK CLACK HOTEL - MEDELLIN. ANTEJARDIN.FOUR SPORT FACILITIES.ORQUIDEORAMA

Each of the twelve projects we present below is explained through a network of ten different circumstances, inscribed in three categories: environmental, social, and voluntary constraints. In the first group of environmental constraints **(EV)**, there are ecological and climatic phenomena, bioclimatic strategies, choice of materials, soil conditions, etc. In the second group of social constraints **(SC)**, there are technological and economic phenomena, construction systems, cultural preferences, political pressures, client and user biases, etc. In the third group of voluntary constraints **(VC)**, there are our variable leanings, often linked to the options opened by the previous restrictions: a geometry, a color, a material, a spatial relationship, a direct connection with the architecture of another author, etc. Although the division we present here is artificial because, in practice, constraints interconnect with each other, it allows us not only to track their origin but also to determine the degree of importance they had in each project. In a general way, we find imposed and intrinsic constraints in the first two categories and self-imposed limitations on the last one. In some cases, we understand the simple choice of color as limitation or self-constraint, but as we will see, even in the face of a group of strong constraints there always seem to be small cracks that allow for proposing some random and subtle features.

In this book, we present our projects through the following documents: constraints network, architectural plans, and performance photographs. All chosen buildings are public or have urban qualities that allowed them to detonate a significant impact in their contexts.

SAN VICENTE COMMUNITY CENTER

CONSTRAINTS NETWORK

SC. Patio and perimeter. The representatives of the Antioquia Government requested us to incorporate spatial and functional strategies expressed in drawings made by the community during some participatory workshops. They repeatedly proposed a perimeter building following the shape of the site, around a courtyard, and a distant visual connection to the church. We started our design from those instructions.

EC. Accurate earthwork. The lot chosen for the construction of the Community center belonged to the municipality. It consisted of a mountain fragment modified for the development of previous interventions (a school, some houses, an unpaved road). The difference in levels between the upper part of the property and its neighbors varied between seven and nine meters. The team of engineers involved in the project, requested the construction of a single-level building, a minimal alteration of the topography, and deep foundations far from the existing slopes.

VC. Public space on the roofs. The commission called for the construction of a small format public space for which there was never enough area on the site. This situation led us to design flat roofs to incorporate new public areas in contact with the distant landscape.

Client: Antioquia Government
Opening: 2016
Program: Civic and educational center + small format public space
Location: San Vicente Ferrer, Antioquia. (Rural area)
Built area: 1,000m²
Ecosystem: Montane wet forest
Altitude above sea level: 2,150 m
Cost per m²: USD 500

SC. Outdoor theater on the ground. Community leaders requested an open-air theater as a novelty to the initial program that suggested a neutral public space. We proposed an edge building with two arms that formed a stand supported on the natural slope of the land and finally contained by the stage. We reviewed the Malaparte house, designed by Adalberto Libera, and built in Capri in 1938 because we remembered that it had an opposite operation through a similar scheme. When we arrive at our building, we go down the trapezoidal stand towards the stage, leaving the everyday landscape above. Upon reaching the house, we climb a trapezoidal staircase that opens to the upper terrace to enjoy the private and unique view.

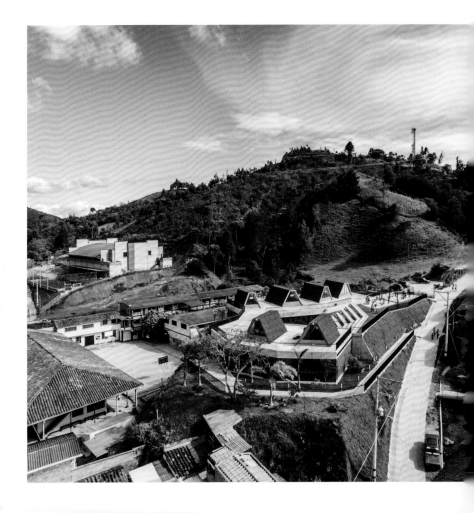

SC. The road as a pedestrian ramp. The regulations requested complete accessibility to the building through ramps with an 8% slope, and this forced us to use the existing secondary road as a connection ramp with the urban fabric of the municipality. From it, we connected two soft ramps: the first one moves along the perimeter of the lot to access the building, and the second one gives access to the roofs and their public spaces (terraces, gardens, and outdoor gym). Both paths connect in a loop through the open-air theater.

VC. Polygonal geometry. For the design of the plan geometry, we decided to follow the logic of the topographic lines near the outer edge of the lot. A first long arm absorbs the polygonal layout of the topography, and a second short arm fits perpendicular to the natural slope of the terrain. In this method we consolidated an edge that contains a stepped void.

EC. Sheltered public space. The tropical and high mountain climate maintain a consistently cold climate. For this reason, we arranged the outdoor theater as a place controlled by the building's internal contours, which cover it laterally from strong wind currents throughout the year.

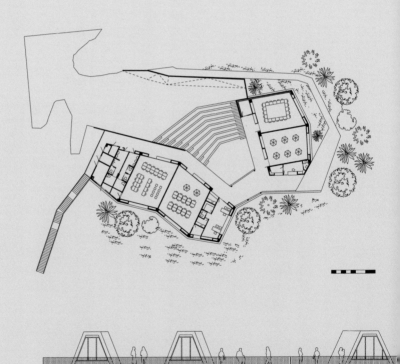

SC. Brown and green. We decided to use materials and colors that are customary in this place, always involving local labor. Rustic brown stone floors and veneers from nearby quarries. Floors in cement tiles, and mineral colors from nearby factories. Ceilings, doors, and wooden baseboards in light green.

EC. No heating. For economic reasons, the building does not have mechanical heating. The bioclimatic design proposed thick walls and materials with high thermal inertia that slowly gain and lose temperature. This strategy conditioned the shape of the walls, the areas of windows, and the characteristics of the concrete roof slab.

SC. Trapezoidal skylights. Government representatives demanded overhead lighting for all four classrooms, the designer in charge of lighting recommended the use of indirect north-south natural light, and the contractor suggested skylights with high rainfall control to avoid future maintenance. In this way, we come to a design of long trapezoidal skylights with protected vertical windows.

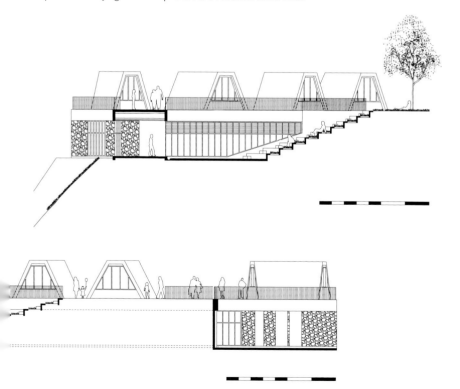

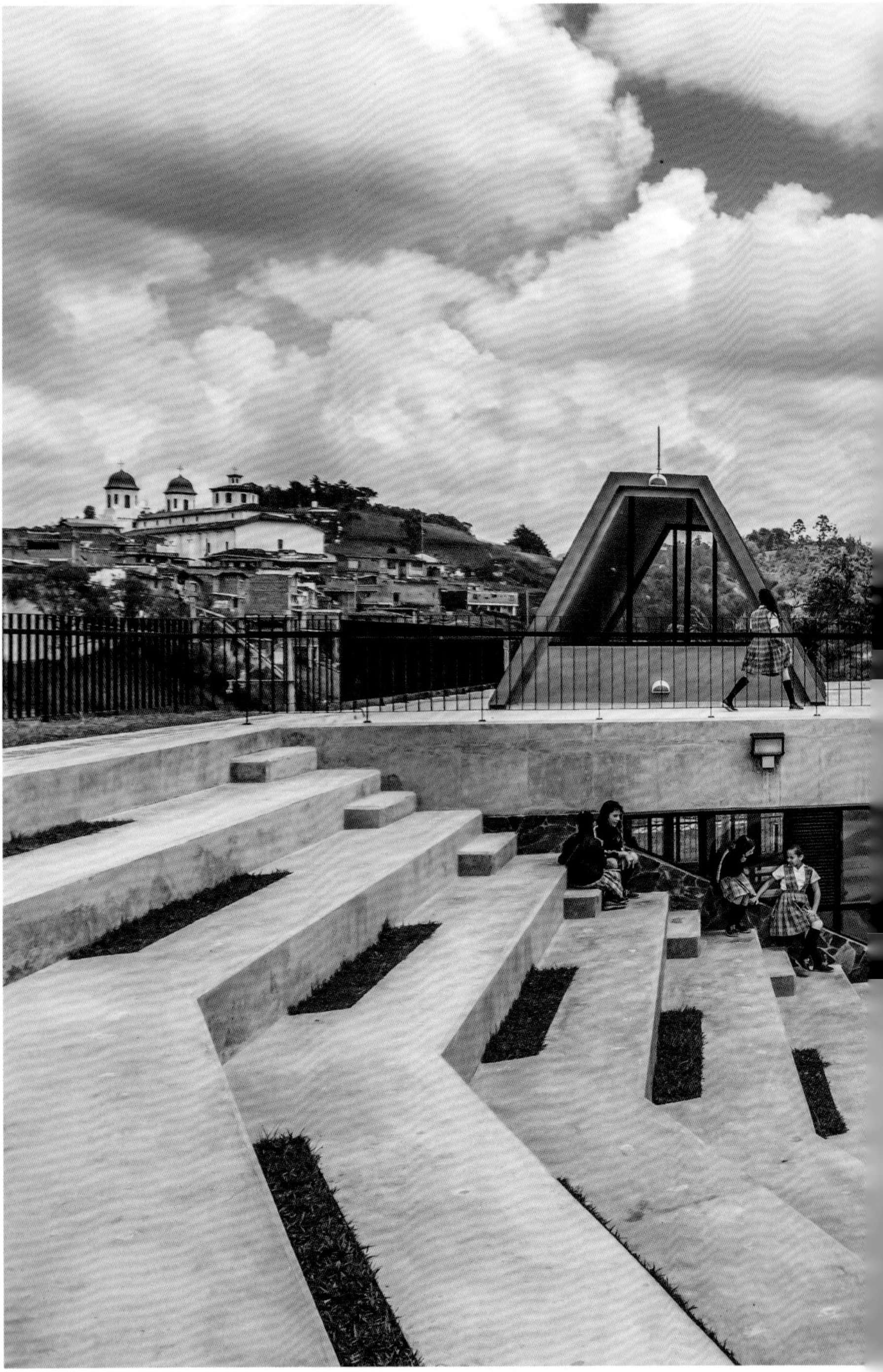

PUERTO TRIUNFO COMMUNITY CENTER

CONSTRAINTS NETWORK

SC. Complete the block. The lot available for the community center was part of a block located on the periphery of a flat and consolidated urban fabric, with precise municipality regulations. The building had to complete the corner of its square, continue the existing facing-wall, and to be a two-story building. The lot was small for the required program, and it was not possible to incorporate an outdoor public space. For this reason, the community requested an ample and flexible space on the first level for cultural activities: cinema, theater, concerts. We located the classrooms and study areas on a secluded and quiet second level.

SC. Structural facade. To have greater flexibility on the ground floor, the representatives of the Antioquia Government, requested to take the structure to the perimeter of the construction. For this reason, we designed the facades as part of the structural system of the building, using tilted columns in two directions providing greater rigidity. In the interior, we only located concrete screens around the rear ramp, thus freeing up an ample interior space.

Client: Antioquia Government
Opening: 2016
Program: Civic and educational center + small format public interior space
Location: Puerto Triunfo, Antioquia. (Rural area)
Built area: 1,140 m²
Ecosystem: Wet tropical forest
Altitude above sea level: 240 m
Cost per m²: USD 500

SC. Minimal maintenance. The municipality requested a resistant, low-maintenance building over time. For this reason, and due to the contribution of cement from a nearby sponsor industry, the building was constructed using exposed concrete, avoiding plaster and paint.

VC. Near ruin. On a previous visit to the site, we came across an abandoned construction, built of concrete blocks. The tropical vegetation had transformed this space into a spontaneous garden of great vitality. We decided to incorporate this environment into our building using rough gray concrete walls, climbing plants on the facades, and large shaded areas.

EC. Solid base. Due to sporadic flooding from the nearby river on the municipality streets, the engineers requested to elevate the project on a solid base. For this reason, the building was built one meter above the level of the outer sidewalks and required a smooth access ramp. This condition generated a closer relationship between the interior spaces and the foliage of the exterior vegetation.

SC. Tropical building. Our client's consultant architect, who also had to approve our final project, recommended developing a permeable and resistant construction in reinforced concrete. He further suggested that we review some similar examples in tropical settings, emphasizing Lecorbusier's Mill Owners' Association Building in Ahmedabad (1954), with its exterior ramp, sunshade facade, and flexible interior space.

EC. Deep facades. Our client requested the design of a
building with bioclimatic qualities instead of using air
conditioning. Faced with a climate with high temperatures
and relative humidity, we proposed a building with deep
and permeable facades, allowing the passage of constant
air currents. For the first level, we designed an almost
transparent metal mesh enclosure, and for the second
one, a concrete block facade with circular perforations. In
this project, the facade works simultaneously as structure,
sunshade, and planter.

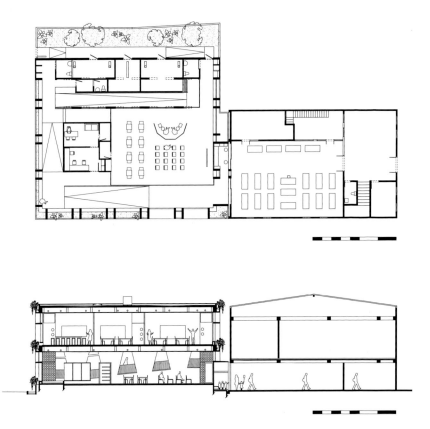

EC. Exempt building. The chosen bioclimatic strategy forced to have a free-standing building with constant cross ventilation. For this, the west and services facade was separated three meters from the neighboring buildings. The north facade maintained a one-meter setback and allowed a new internal connection to a cultural building. And the east and south facades shaped the corner of the block, consolidating the growth of the existing urban fabric.

SC. Internal ramp. In compliance with the current regulations, we proposed a ramp in three sections with an 8% slope, located at the west end of the building. Due to its large size in proportion to the total project area, we understood it as an extra space for recreational activities and not only as an efficient and safe circulation. The spaciousness and comfort conditions of this ramp avoided the need to build stairs.

VC. Green and Orange. We chose a soft green color for the floors and ceilings and a bright orange color for the handrails and facade bars.

SANTO DOMINGO KINDERGARTEN

CONSTRAINTS NETWORK

VC. Pentagons. This commission arose from a competition we previously won, in which the brief was to design a kindergarten adaptable to different lots. On that occasion, we proposed a modular strategy that allowed us to adapt the program and the shape of the building to changing places and topographies. In this case, our client asked us for a similar strategy. For this, we used pentagonal modules with size variations that allowed us to move flexibly inside an irregular lot.

EC. Shallow earthmoving. Faced with the prohibition of using dynamite (due to city security regulations) and the economic impossibility of implementing chemical products to break large existing rocks in the ground, we decided to adapt the building to the natural slope of the terrain, which allowed for the earthworks carried out to be small.

VC. Non-imposing building. To adapt the new construction to an irregular and diverse urban fabric, we proposed a configuration of changing levels, corners, terraces, ramps, and roofs; also, a singular and recognizable building in the middle of a neighborhood with low income and material diversity. We tried not to arrive to the place with a new imposing configuration, but with a subtle and dynamic construction.

Client: Buen comienzo. Municipality of Medellin
Opening: 2011
Program: Kindergarten
Location: Santo Domingo Savio, Medellin
Built area: 1,500 m²
Ecosystem: Montane forest
Altitude above sea level: 1,800 m
Cost per m²: USD 700

SC. Head and tail. The mayor's office representatives requested a program with differentiated areas. The lot shape led us to propose a "head" with a patio for the children, and a "tail" with a terrace for the teenagers.

EC. Permeable patio. We decided to remove some pentagonal modules from the program to open the patio to the daily life of the neighborhood and the distant landscape. Although the spring climate of the city of Medellin does not require the use of air conditioning, we proposed subtle bioclimatic strategies to achieve comfortable environments throughout the year: cross ventilation in all classrooms, deep facades, vertical brise soleils, and covered walkways.

SC. Uneven ramps. We proposed a system of irregular ramps adapted to the topography of the site, connecting the lower level of the street, the intermediate level of the patio, and the upper level of the classrooms. This route allows the stepped solution of the building.

SC. Blue and green. The mayor of Medellin's wife, indirectly involved in this project, suggested that the building needed colors: blue and green. We recommended not to apply paint, thinking of the high wear and future maintenance, but rather incorporate mineral color to the granite plaster mix used on the facade. Blue is a widely used color in this neighborhood where self-construction is normal, and it symbolizes that the inhabitants completed a building that was in process for some time.

VC. No fences. To avoid perimeter fences and simultaneously consolidate a safe building for children but close to the community, we proposed a control base in direct contact with the street, and an isolated second level with the classrooms. Only at the rear of the construction, where part of the program comes into contact with the terrain, we designed a fence accompanied by slopes and gardens.

SC. Available building. The first level of the "head" — patio, services, rooms — works independently and can be isolated from the rest of the project. In this way, the community — elders, community leaders, mothers' associations — can partially use the kindergarten during the weekends, expanding the use of the building.

EC. Tunnels and mounds. Responding to a limited budget, the contractor proposed to build the necessary playground equipment, using the remaining material from the earthworks. Considering his suggestion, we designed tunnels and mounds covered with grass and surrounded them with native vegetation.

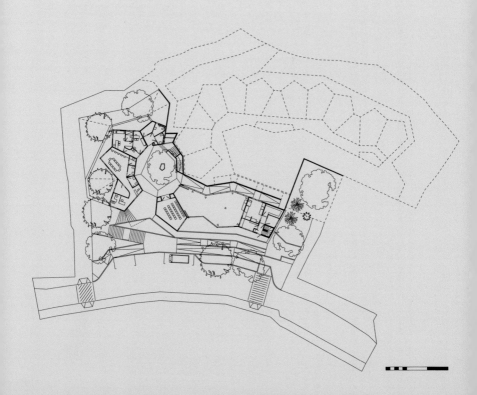

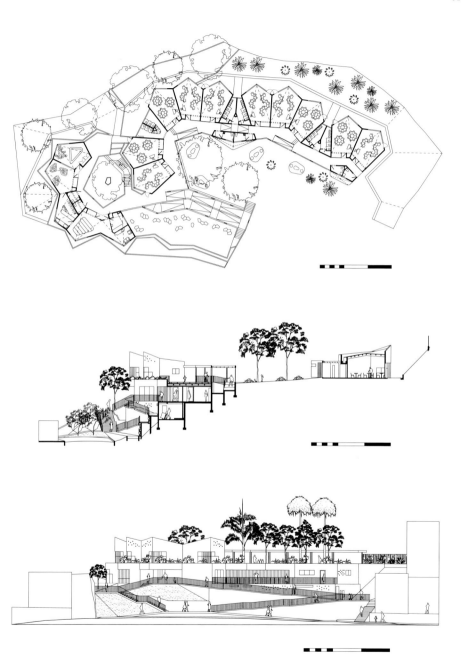

EMBERA SCHOOL

CONSTRAINTS NETWORK

EC. Stilt structure. This isolated municipality, located on the banks of the Atrato River, floods several times a year during the seasons of heavy rain cycle. The existing constructions are stilt buildings prepared for that phenomenon. The client asked us for a reinforced concrete lower structure, resistant and elevated above the maximum level of historical flooding. They also requested to connect the new construction to the existing urban fabric of elevated pedestrian walkways.

EC. Lightweight building. Faced with a low resistance of the soil, the structural engineer requested us to design a light, single-level building. He proposed a foundation system consisting of 80 concrete micro-piles connected to the floor platform columns. From this level on, he suggested the use of light and prefabricated metal structure.

SC. Boat transportation. Vigia del Fuerte is a place surrounded by jungles and is connected to the country by light aircraft and small ships. For this reason, we defined the structural and architectural modules — beams, columns, wooden elements — of the building, according to the capacity of the available boats.

Client: Fundacion Fraternidad Medellin
Opening: 2014
Program: Native community School
Location: Vigia del Fuerte, Antioquia. (Rural area)
Built area: 1,305 m²
Ecosystem: Humid tropical forest
Altitude above sea level: 18 m
Cost per m²: USD 700

EC. Wood. The native Embera community requested a construction with a significant wood component. Because the use of native and nearby woods is prohibited (most species are at risk of extinction), we decided to use Patula pinewood extracted from certified tree crops near Medellin. We designed all the enclosures, and the main walls of the building using this light and resistant wood.

SC. Traditional typology. The representatives of the government requested the architecture to be similar to the local example, with gabled roofs and large eaves to protect from the constant rains. The native community asked us to avoid designing a building, which would be strange for their traditional logics. Therefore, we proposed a rectangular building, consisting of three longitudinal roofs, with two long internal gutters and perimeter eaves. To remind of the typical indigenous *Malokas* (communal building with a big roof), we conceived the building as a grouping of long roofs, with flexible interiors for various uses.

VC. Covered street. We organized the program into three parallel bars. On the edges, we located classrooms, bedrooms, service areas, and offices. In the middle, we left a flexible covered street for the events requested by the native community: classes, parties, ceremonies. Because native students come to the municipality 15 days a month and then return to their houses in the jungle, this building works simultaneously as a school, home, and public space.

EC. Stands and piers. We designed docks on the main facades of the building to connect it to daily boat activities during the flood season. To articulate the change in level between the piers and the interior of the school, we proposed stands that allow people to wait and observe the nearby landscape.

EC. No air-conditioning. Due to a humid and hot tropical climate, budget limitations, and the impossibility of having constant electric power, our client requested a permeable and cross-ventilated building for all its spaces. We proposed frame wood facades, windows without glass but with mosquito nets, and vertical wood blinds. We even designed perforations for the base of the reinforced concrete floor to take advantage of surface wind currents.

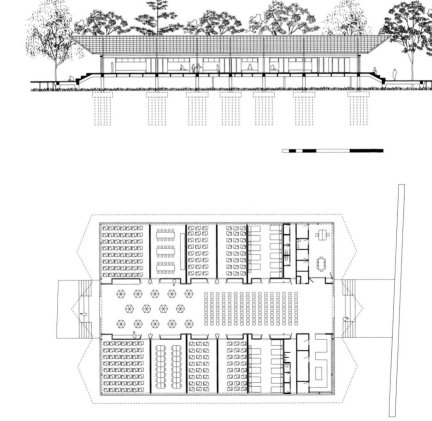

SC. Exposed structure. Initially, we designed wooden ceilings to soften the perception of the interior space and control the level of the temperature. Anyhow, due to budgetary restrictions, the client requested to eliminate them. For this reason, the entire metal structure and the roofs with their translucent stripes have a strong presence inside the building.

VC. Green, white and red. We proposed green roofs to camouflage the building in the jungle context. Following instructions from the Colombian army (who watch over this area affected by violence), we changed to white as it was easy to recognize and control. We proposed the use of a reddish mineral for the construction of the concrete floor, and green to paint the doors and the wooden baseboards.

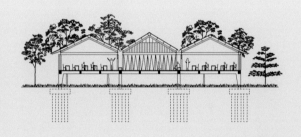

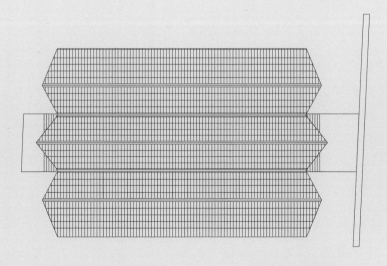

SIETE VUELTAS SCHOOL

CONSTRAINTS NETWORK

SC. Modularity. Due to transport and economic limitations, our client requested a design based on the repetition of a structural and constructive module with repeated measures and materials: reinforced concrete structure, concrete block enclosures, and a roof supported on a light metal secondary structure.

VC. Dirt road. Due to the proximity of a noisy, dusty, and unpaved road, we proposed to build most of the school in a wide internal area, surrounded by vegetation. This way, the school connects to the existing urban fabric through the administrative module and a small sports field that can be used by the entire community during the weekends.

SC. Existing soccer field. Our client requested us to keep an existing soccer field in the internal area of the lot, therefore, we chose to disperse the program in small modular buildings around the play areas. This ample open space is used intensively by the educational community during the study and recess hours. The buildings are connected through an internal covered corridor, leaving open trapezoidal separations on the outside.

Client: Fundacion Fraternidad Medellin
Opening: 2015
Program: School
Location: San Juan de Uraba, Antioquia. (rural area)
Built area: 1,776 m²
Ecosystem: Dry tropical forest
Altitude above sea level: 2 m
Cost per m²: USD 700

SC. Restaurant as a flexible space. Due to education regulations, the restaurant area functions as an open space for various events: concerts, theater, meetings, etc. The program did not include a specific area for theater or music, instead of a multiuse and flexible space for cultural events, connected to the office building and close to the entrance.

SC. Sponsoring companies. Our client suggested using cement, concrete blocks, and mineral colors from local sponsoring companies. We implemented these products on the main structure of the building, on the concrete floors, and all the walls.

EC. Secondary structure. Due to the low resistance of the soil, engineers suggested constructing single-level, lightweight buildings. Because we implemented a reinforced concrete general structure, they requested us to design a secondary structure using metal beams to support the roofs and light eaves.

EC. Cross ventilation. Due to cultural conditions and economic restrictions, and faced with a dry and warm climate, the client requested us to design a building without air conditioning and with cross ventilation in all its spaces. For this reason, we created a horizontal gap between the roofs and the enclosure walls, allowing hot air to escape. We also proposed walls built with perforated concrete blocks.

VC. Brown and orange. We decided to use the cheapest colors offered in the concrete block catalog: dark brown, light brown, and orange. According to this color range, we kept the natural rusty color for the main metal beams, and we chose orange for the secondary beams and metal bars.

VC. Future covered pathways. The restricted budget did not allow for the construction of two covered walkways that we designed to create shade and divide the large interior patio into three zones: two playgrounds at the ends and the soccer field in the middle. We finished the design of these structures so that the municipality can build them in the future.

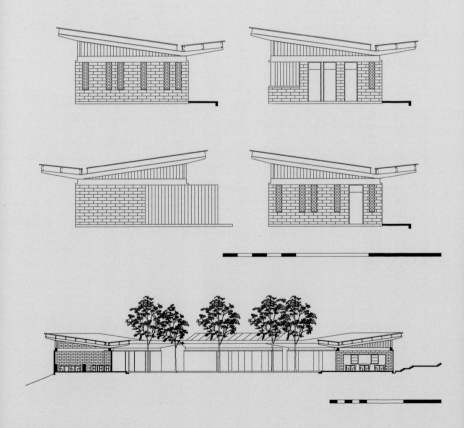

EC. Water tank towers. Due to intermittent water service in the area, the hydraulic engineer requested the design of two towers to support water storage tanks. We designed these structures using fragments left over from the metal structure of the roofs, and we located them at the ends of the outer perimeter of the patio.

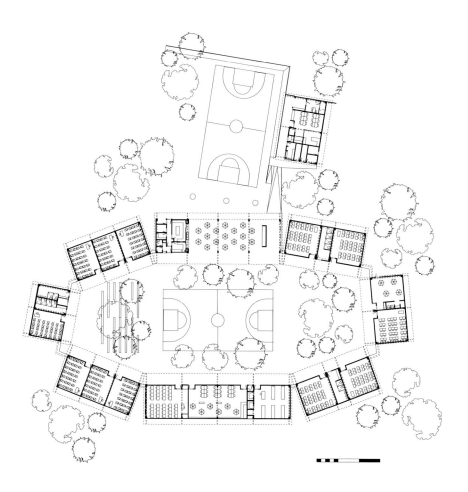

JARDIN SCHOOL

EC. Strips of stable ground. The purpose of this commission was to replace existing buildings in poor conditions and respond with a new project to an unstable and low resistance terrain. We designed the new buildings on the strips of stable ground defined by the soil engineer. In conversations with the school principal, we determined three major program zones in this large rural lot: the lower part for the high school, the upper part for the middle school, and the intermediate zone with a geological fault in the middle, only for walkways and gardens.

VC. Concave/Convex. We defined the longitudinal and extended shape of the new constructions not only according to the strips of stable ground but also to the need to preserve the existing sports fields. In the lower area of the lot, we located the building on the outer perimeter of the existing terrace, configuring a large playground employing a concave geometry. In the upper area, we located the building on the inner edge of the existing terrace, through a convex geometry that opened up to the landscape.

Client: Fundacion Fraternidad Medellin
Opening: 2016
Program: School
Location: Jardin, Antioquia. (rural area)
Built area: 1,543 m²
Ecosystem: Montane forest
Altitude above sea level: 1,750 m
Cost per m²: USD 700

EC. Low constructions. The structural conditions of the terrain led us to design light, single-level buildings. The soil engineer proposed concrete floating slabs for the foundations, distributing the structural loads in a balanced way on the ground.

SC. Concrete Structure. In conversation with the structural engineer, we decided to use a simple reinforced concrete structure, with slightly inclined tie beams, supporting metal joists, and a lightweight roof. In the corridor area, the concrete structure is cantilevered, and in the opposite facade, the columns act as sun breakers at a slight angle. The gap between the main beams and the secondary edge beams, receive the roof and the rainwater gutters.

SC. Protected corridors. The principal of the school asked us to make the corridors a bit independent of the outdoor sports activities. For this, we proposed intermittent panels with low-cost metal meshes, accompanied by climbing and native plants. In high school, the hallways surround the playground, at the middle school, the corridors open to the landscape. In both cases, we used the same architectural section but inverted.

VC. Mountainous landscape. These buildings are also a route along the rugged terrain. Its users access through a smooth ramp that leads to the high school playground. From there, they walk along the corridor of the first building and then carry on along an open path, connected to the middle school and its spacious terrace.

EC. Passive strategies. The spring climate of this municipality does not require the use of air conditioning. Anyhow, it does need some passive strategies to reach a comfortable built environment: cross ventilation in all its spaces, deep shady facades, and sun breakers controlling the afternoon sun.

VC. Brown, orange, white. In contrast to the range of greens present in the nearby gardens and the distant landscape, we chose to use earthy colors for the building: brown for the blocks and floors, and orange for the bars of the windows, and metal panels. Our client wanted white tiles for the roofs because they are always in stock.

EC. Orchard. The original topographical condition of the high school terrace presented a small sinking that allowed us to build a short fragment of the building in a basement. In this way, we connected three new classrooms directly to the outdoor orchards.

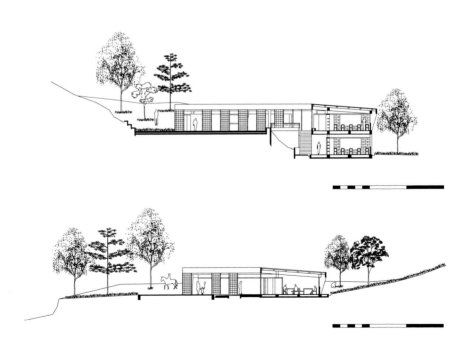

VC. Distant marks. In this rural and agricultural area with very few constructions, we understood the new educational buildings as clearly visible marks in the landscape. Delicate but unique.

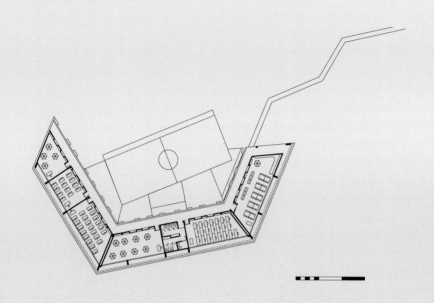

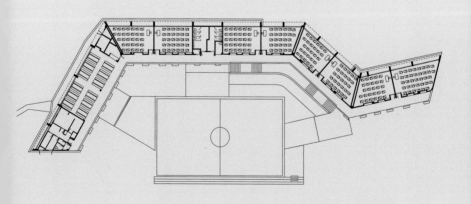

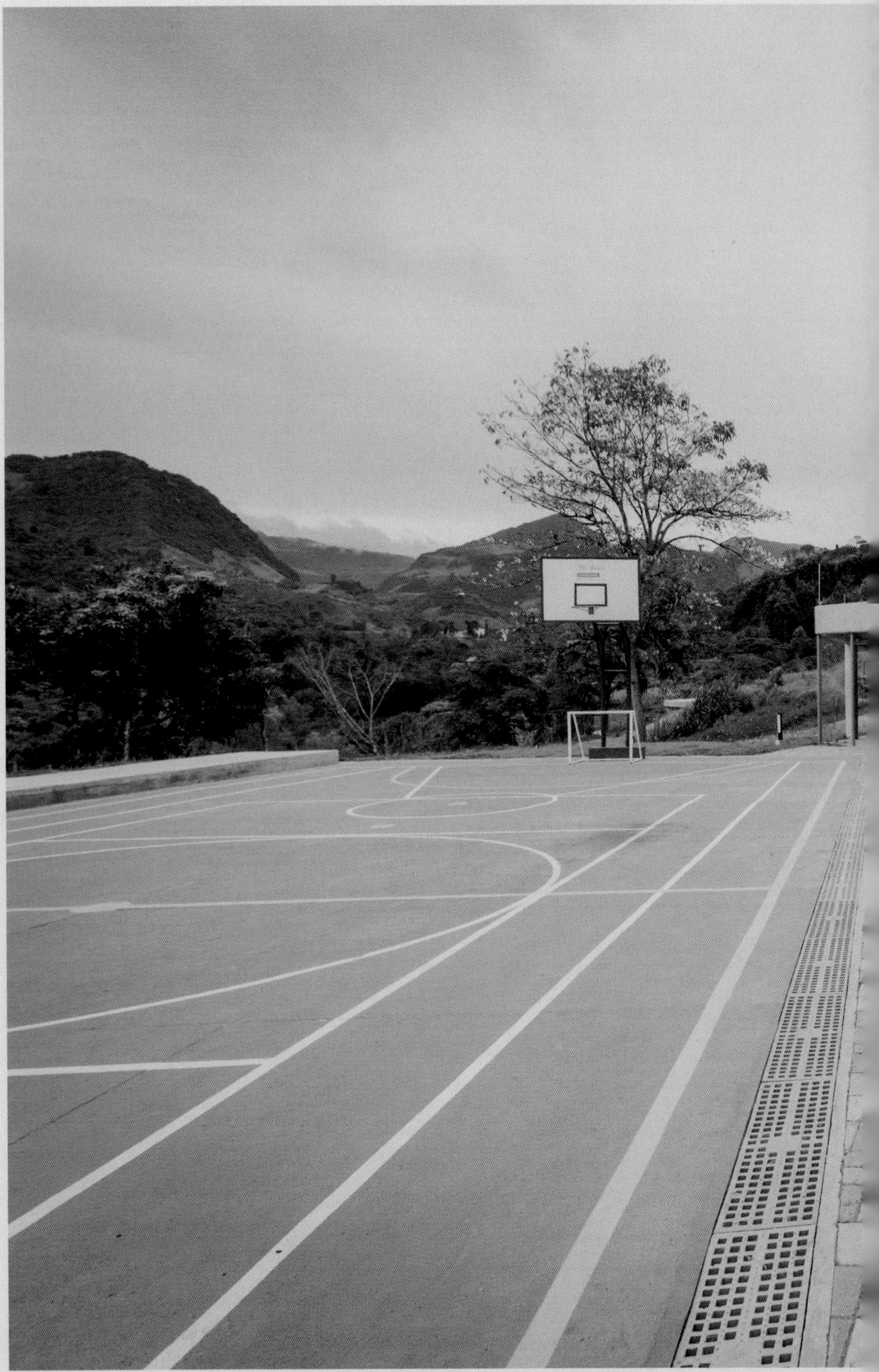

SAN VICENTE SCHOOL

CONSTRAINTS NETWORK

SC. Elongated building. After demolishing an old building that did not meet current Colombian seismic resistance codes, our client requested the design of a new school, located on the extended footprint of the previous one, because it was occupying the only stable land on the lot.

VC. No fence to the street. To continue occupying the footprint of the former construction and leave more space for sports and games areas, we moved the position of the new building to the southern limit of the lot. In this way, we not only replicated its polygonal footprint and built a new enclosure, but we avoided having to construct a future fence towards the street.

SC. Two opposite facades. In this building, we designed two different facades. The first one, towards a dusty and noisy road, is closed and hermetic. The second one, towards a distant rural landscape, is open and porous. For the first case, we designed a closed polygonal wall, with a few rectangular windows. For the second, we created large windows and located the corridors that function as balconies and viewpoints.

SC. Simple structure. The budget restrictions determined the choice of a straightforward reinforced concrete structure (columns, beams, slabs, and marquee). To support the roof, we designed a secondary light structure using parallel metal beams. The marquee covering the upper hallway also supports eight small water storage tanks.

Client: Fundacion Fraternidad Medellin.
Opening: 2015
Program: Middle School
Location: San Vicente, Antioquia. (Rural area)
Built area: 995 m²
Ecosystem: Humid montane forest
Altitude above sea level: 2,150 m
Cost per m²: USD 700

SC. Normal windows. The facade towards the street seemed very hard for a school, for that reason, we explored different types of windows: cantilevered volumes, eaves, concrete frames, etc. But on this occasion, our client was strict with his expectations: he only wanted rectangular openings and simple metal bars. Therefore, we proposed a limited number of windows with metal bars replicating the pattern of the facade block.

EC. Changing Perimeter. The soil engineer requested us to encircle the existing sports field built on unstable ground. For this reason, we designed the school as a built perimeter with different thicknesses.

VC. Ramp/stairs. Responding to the program, we proposed a two-story building: downstairs the kindergarten, library, restaurant, and service areas. Upstairs, the middle school classrooms and offices. On the east end, we used the ramp shape part of the building enclosure, which avoided covering the landscape. At the narrow west end, we located a compact staircase, consolidating the games terrace.

EC. Compact configuration. The cold, tropical, and rainy climate of this mountainous area does not require a heating system. Anyhow, simple passive strategies bring comfort. The main facade is facing the afternoon sun in a diagonal angle, the concrete slabs and blocks have high thermal inertia, losing and gaining temperature slowly, and the building has an elongated but compact configuration.

VC. Gray, Brown, red, yellow. We decided to use concrete blocks in an inexpensive range of five colors: dark gray, dark brown, red, light brown, and yellow. In the closed facade, we designed this set of changing tones to try and the aspect of the long wall. For all metal elements — doors, beams, bars, and railings — we chose yellow.

SC. New Roof. Two years after inaugurating the building, our client requested us to design a roof for the sports field, to carry out events during the endless rainy hours. In this case, we created a light metal structure with deep foundations and connected to the second level concrete marquee. In this way, we avoided covering the distant rural landscape, incorporating a new rectangular structure, foreign to the existing geometry.

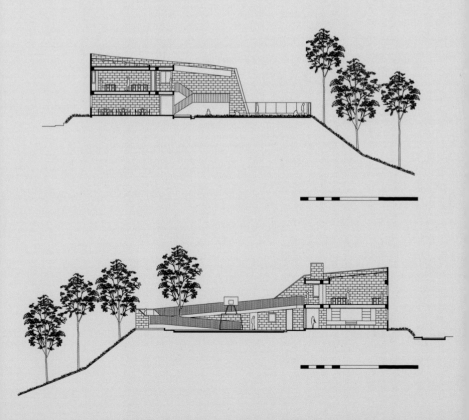

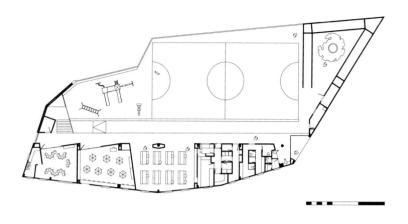

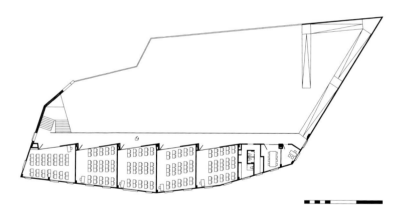

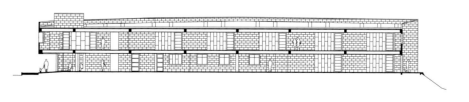

HONTANARES SCHOOL

CONSTRAINTS NETWORK

EC. Geographical features. Faced with a very sloping and irregular rural lot, we arranged the program according to the characteristics of the various geographic features: classrooms on the side slopes, the restaurant on the central hill, open area, and schoolyard on the central plateau, and sports area in the dip. We defined the most advantageous position for each activity of the school, using the topographic possibilities of the terrain.

SC. Central plateau. We proposed not to build on the central plateau to have an open place in which to gather all the children of the school. This decision led us to arrange the buildings throughout the lot, encouraging the children and teachers to walk and enjoy the scenery. If you are small you are close to the native forest, if you are ten years old you are close to the hillside with fruit trees, if you are a teenager, you are close to the sports pit, and when you meet with others, you are on the central plateau.

EC. Long terrace. By avoiding constructing a compact multi-level building on the plateau, we were forced to design careful earthworks, following the geometry of the topographic lines. Recalling the traditional Chinese terraced rice fields, we decided to make moderate cuts and fillings, setting up a narrow terrace along the lot, bordering the central plateau, in an east to west direction.

Client: Evolucionar S.A.S.
Design partner: Alejandro Bernal
Opening: 2005 (Competition 2003)
Program: School
Location: El Retiro, Antioquia
Built area: 4,000 m²
Ecosystem: Humid montane forest
Altitude above sea level: 2,420 m
Cost per m²: USD 500

SC. No obstacles. The educational strategy of this school is inclusive of children with physical disabilities. Therefore, it was imperative to design a horizontal building without stairs. To do this, we connected the upper level of the plateau, with the lower level of the classrooms through ramps. The children begin their journey in the lobby connected to the parking lot, make use of the plateau, descend the ramps, and move along the lower terrace without obstacles or steps.

SC. Changing phases. Our client requested a design planned in stages, which could be arranged on anticipated earthworks, to generate provisional play terraces and allow for orderly growth. Stage one, on the west terrace and central area: fifteen classrooms, bathrooms, library, covered ramp, restaurant, and provisional offices. Stage two, on the east terrace and central area: five classrooms, four teachers' rooms, bathrooms, expansion of the restaurant, and a second ramp connected to the covered hall. Stage three (the future phase), on the eastern terrace: four classrooms and a new library. The construction phases underwent constant changes and modifications that we adapted to the changing needs and budgetary reality of the school.

VC. Flat roofs. Although our clients requested buildings with high and traditional roofs, we proposed flat terraces for the roofs of the main constructions that surround the central plateau. In this way, we extended the usable flat area and avoided covering the view of the distant landscape. These buildings function as edges connected to the plateau through a bridge, and the students use the roofs as recreational areas.

SC. Rectangular modules. Due to the curved and diagonal geometry of the terraces and economic and technical limitations, we proposed to repeat and move rectangular modules, adapting them to the sinuous shape and avoiding the construction of curves. In section, these modules fill the space left by the earthworks without touching the rear slopes and have roofs with three variable inclinations, following the natural slope of the mountain. On that occasion, we reviewed the Vigo University Campus classroom building, designed by Carmen Pinós and Enric Miralles (2003), in which they located five rectangular boxes, adapted to a curved circulation.

VC. Boomerangs. To connect the classroom modules and provide a covered corridor, we proposed flat concrete roofs, in the form of extensive boomerangs tracing the geometry of the topographic lines. The first one, concave and of greater length, contains the landscape of the nearby native forest. The second one, convex and shorter, opens up to the distant rural view. Initially, we designed native pinewood ceilings for these areas, but due to budget limitations, they were removed during the construction, exposing a rough concrete surface.

VC. Yellow, orange, brown, red, and green. We chose inexpensive and low-maintenance materials: concrete blocks, thermoacoustic roof-tiles, and cement floor tiles. Trying to get closer to the color palette of the reddish tropical soil, we selected yellow, brown, orange, and red materials. Attempting to amplify the color of the grass in the interior spaces, we designed windows with transparent and green etched glass.

SC. Uneven lobby. Due to the rainy climate of the place, during the second phase of construction, we were asked to design a covered hall, connecting the access ramps and giving way to the central plateau. For this, we used the same materials and construction system of the existing ramp (solid exposed concrete slabs and circular metal columns), incorporating the irregular geometry of the available area.

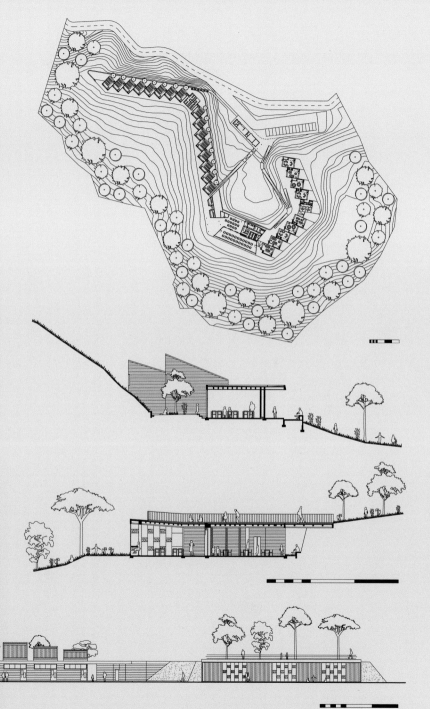

CLICK CLACK HOTEL - MEDELLIN

CONSTRAINTS NETWORK

VC. Perforated block. Our client purchased two adjacent lots on the same block: the first one crossing in a south-north direction, and the second one shaping the north-east corner. By demolishing the existing buildings, the possibility of generating urban connections within the square became evident. Our client proposed a hotel that offered open spaces to the city (in a controlled manner), that also functioned as a center for cultural events (musical, gastronomic, artistic, and festive events). Therefore, we proposed a system of porous urban spaces on the ground floor: passage, patio, stands, terraces, stage, and lobbies, accompanied by restaurants, art gallery, cafe, and a basement for loud parties.

SC. Regulations. Two similar urban regulations defined the general shape of the building. For the whole block, a maximum ground floor height of 5 meters and a 70% maximum construction area of the lot. The south side block allowed a maximum height of 8 stories and an 11-meter setback separating the road axis to the facade. The north side of the block had a 5-story maximum height restriction and 9.50-11-meter setbacks to the road axis. In this way, we designed a building with different overhangs depending on the height and position.

Client: Monkey Business S.A.S.
Opening: 2019
Program: Hotel
Location: Medellin
Built area: 8,723 m^2
Ecosystem: Montane forest
Altitude above sea level: 1,600 m
Cost per m^2: USD 1,300

SC. Capsules. Our client defined this hotel as the articulation of habitable capsules of different sizes (between 15 and 70 m²) for different kinds of visitors. They supported that simple idea on their review of some cases such as the famous Nagakin Capsule Tower, designed by Kisho Kurokawa in Tokyo (1972). Although we did not explore prefabrication and assembly, the ideas of modularity and flexibility were relevant for the design of the first hotel in Bogota (2014), and this second building. The tropical climate of Medellin not only led us to separate the volumes, introducing natural light and cross ventilation between them but also to better them employing balconies, terraces, gardens, staircases, and practicable windows.

SC. Metal structure. Our client needed to build this structure quickly to obtain government tax exemptions for hotels built before 2020. For this reason, the engineers recommended the use of a large-span, fast-building metal structure. Following the suggestion of the client, we decided to expose a large number of connections, braces, bolts, and structural elements inside the rooms and on the building facades.

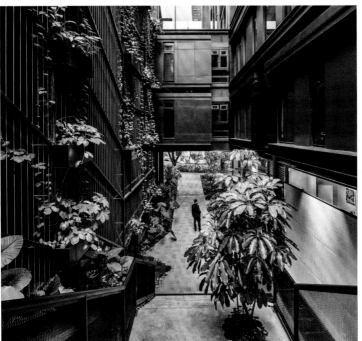

EC. Air-conditioned rooms. Although Medellin's spring weather has generated a local culture that does not require the use of air conditioning, foreign tourists often ask for it. Thus, the hotel has air-conditioned capsules, but the common spaces — hallways, bathrooms, restaurants, lobbies, etc. — are passively controlled and allow constant contact with the mild climate of the city.

SC. Open terraces. After extensive discussions with some representatives of the municipality, we were allowed to locate everyday programs on the rooftops but always using light pergolas: gym, restaurant, bar, swimming pool, outdoor cinema, etc.

SC. Affordable materials. Due to the high costs of the metal structure, our client decided that the other materials of the building should be simple. We proposed black and gray pavers for sidewalks and outside floor, cast concrete for benches, stands and stage, and flat metal sheet facade veneer. At the request of the structural engineer, we designed all the interior partitions using lightweight and flexible gypsum boards, allowing for future changes in an agile way.

SC. Fixed Furniture. For the interior design of the hotel, our client put together an internal team of designers that he could direct carefully. In this way, our work was limited to the interior design of fixed furniture (bathrooms, kitchens, counters, showers, cabinets, etc.) for which we proposed metal structures and transparent glass enclosures, avoiding reducing the limited space of the rooms. We made a subtle accompaniment for the choice of furniture and interior finishes.

SC. Graphite gray. After many tests and combinations, our client decided to use one color for the entire exterior of the building: graphite gray. He based his argument on the idea of understanding the structure as a large monochromatic submarine or metal bridge. In contrast to the volumetric movement of the building, the use of a single color that produced a neutral effect of darkness and shadow seemed unexpected.

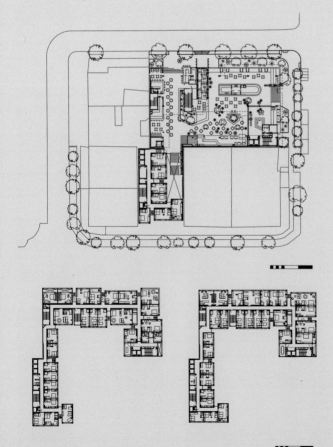

VC. Tropical vegetation. In collaboration with the landscape architects Epífita, we proposed wild and dense landscaping. We used more than 50 species of native plants with a wide variety of features. Wildlife attracting plants, aromatic, climbing, and hanging plants that we combined according to their position: front gardens, terraces, dividing walls, balconies, etc.

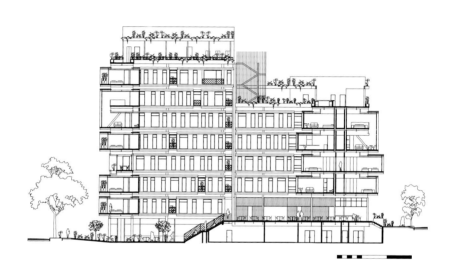

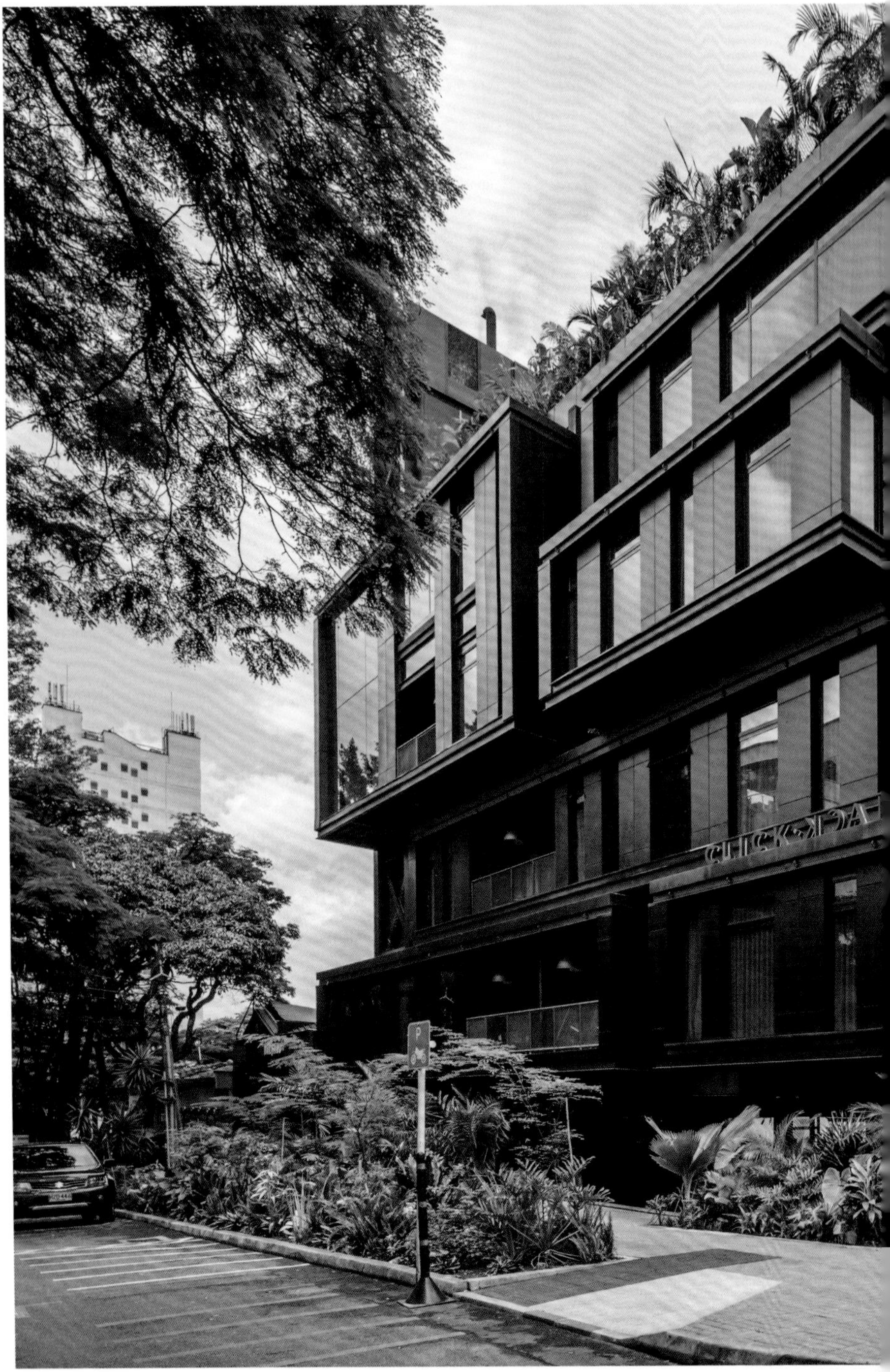
P

CONSTRAINTS NETWORK

VC. Corner building. To consolidate a traditional urban fabric of long blocks, we strengthen the idea of the building as a new corner. In this way, we took all the built mass to the external perimeter of the lot, leaving an interior patio. Faced with a neighborhood that adapts to new urban regulations that allows higher buildings, this construction could function as a modest guideline for future developments. We proposed a smoothed and curved corner to accompany the daily pedestrian movement. During the design process, we remembered "Bonjour Tristesse," the beautiful housing project designed by Álvaro Siza Vieira built in the eighties in Berlin, which not only completed the corner of the block using a broad curve but incorporated the rhythms and perforations of adjacent buildings.

SC. Overhang. The municipal regulation of this area of the city defined relevant aspects of the building: 8 stories maximum height, 5.5 meters ground level height, a 70-80% maximum construction area of the lot, and setbacks separating the main facades and the surrounding roads of 10 meters for levels 2 and 3 and 11 meters for the other levels. Thus, the new volume generates a first shaded access covered by two upper cantilevered levels.

Client: Mensula — Trazos Urbanos
Opening: 2020
Program: Office building
Location: Medellin
Built area: 8,000 m²
Ecosystem: Montane forest
Altitude above sea level: 1,600 m
Cost per m²: USD 900

VC. Branched columns. The east facade of the building has a low commercial strip in connection with the street. The first level of the south facade moves back, generating a covered space in direct contact with the hall and the interior patio. In this area, we designed three-branched concrete columns that our client accepted after a long process of discussion. We argued that we wanted to connect the structure of the lower part of the building with the outdoor garden center.

EC. Nursery. The proximity of the new building with a large nursery of native plants posed the challenge of incorporating this botanical diversity along all the facades. After a lengthy discussion with our client, he finally agreed to this idea, arguing that green facades were in fashion. The landscape designer proposed a wild design, using more than 40 native botanical species, arranged around the facade planters, the terraces, and the front gardens of the building.

SC. Smooth Curves. We understood the entire building as a large corner generated by soft curves. At the tip, we use a fragment of a curve with a 3 meter radius. On the exterior facades, we connected straight lines through 30-meter radius curves avoiding the loss of usable interior area and adapting to a narrow movement range.

EC. Shady Facades. The spring weather of Medellin does not require the use of air conditioning. In this case, we proposed simple bioclimatic strategies: metal sunscreens located on the facades facing the afternoon sun and randomly positioned, deep and shady facades, and cross ventilation in all interior spaces.

SC. Stepped terraces. The municipal regulation allowed having terraces towards the inner courtyard. In this way, the building is stepped and widens as it approaches the lower part of the lot, incorporating gardens and opening up to the distant view of the city.

SC. Precast gray concrete edges. For the facade edges that shape the planters, we proposed cast concrete walls with vertical grooves looking for a gray monolithic and resistant appearance. After conducting various tests with the builder, our client considered that the best option in terms of appearance and speed of construction was the use of lightweight, modular precast concrete panels. In this method, the curves became slightly polygonal, and the presence became less heavy.

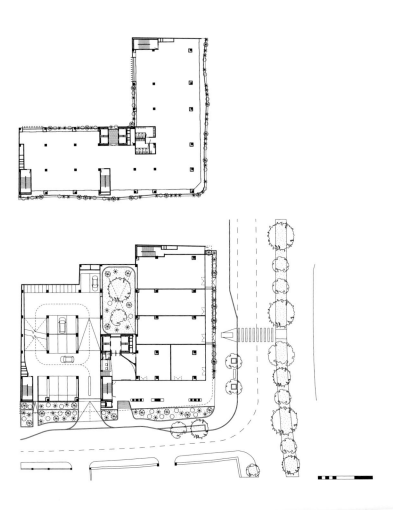

SC. Flexible Space. Our clients conceived this building as a generic office property to rent to different private companies. They requested a flexible open-plan and large sliding glass doors on the perimeter. The only elements that alter this layout are the three mandatory evacuation stairs, the shared bathrooms, and a small hall with four elevators.

SC. Parking areas. Budgetary limitations and structural soil conditions only allowed the construction of two parking basements. To reach the required parking area, we proposed two extra floors above the access level. This situation, permitted by municipal regulations, shaped a building where terraces, balconies, gardens, patio, and overhangs, strive to cover and blur the vehicular areas.

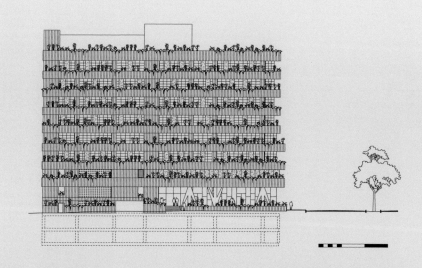

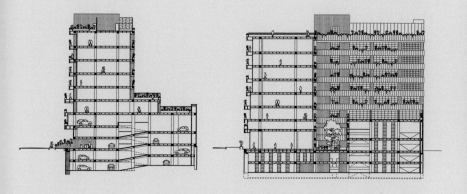

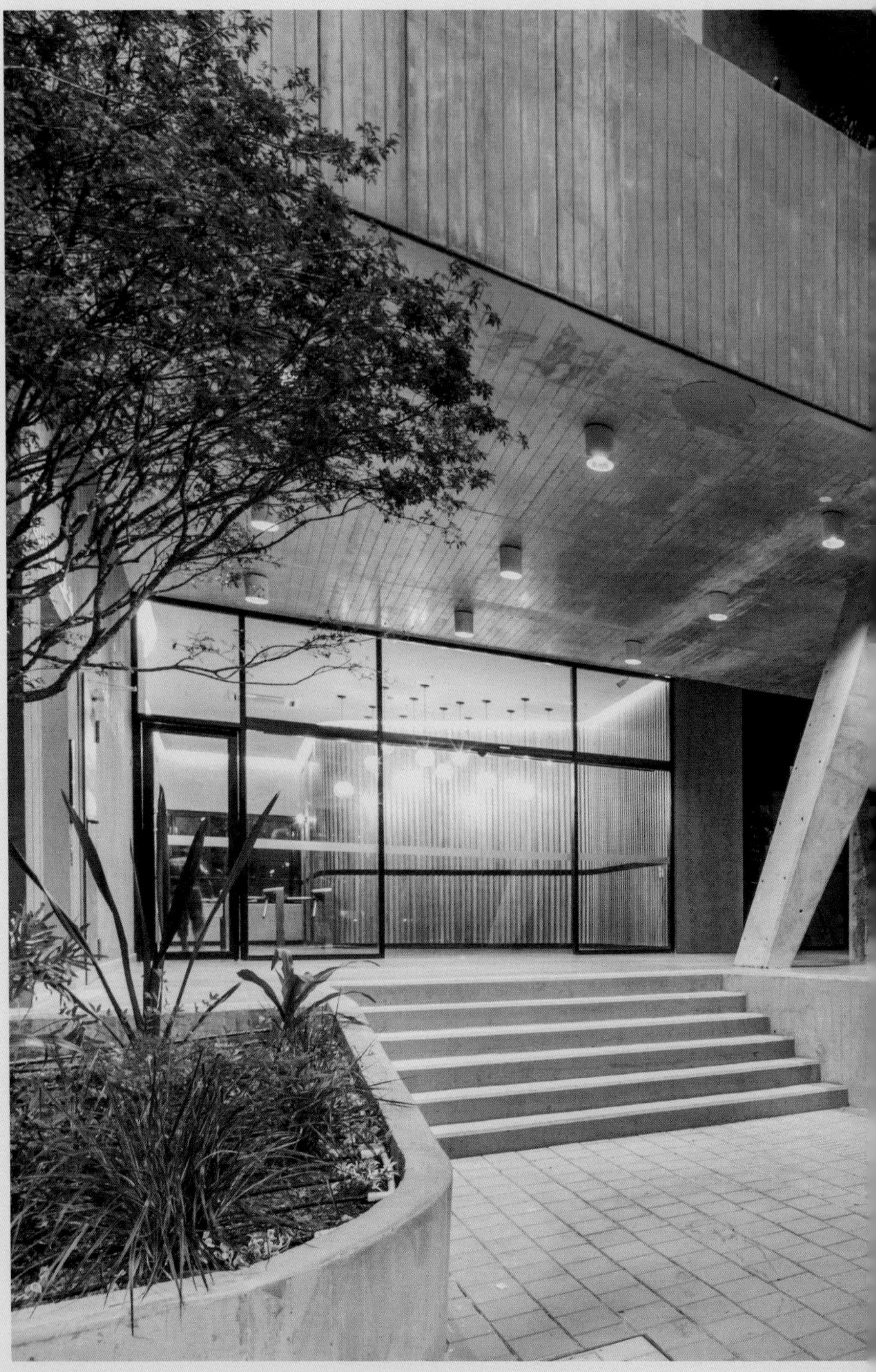

FOUR SPORT FACILITIES

CONSTRAINTS NETWORK

SC. Built Continent. To host the 2010 South American Games in Medellin, the mayor's office opened a public competition to design three buildings (volleyball, combat, and olympic gymnastics) and remodel the existing basketball building. The area intended for these new constructions consisted of a restricted fragment of the Medellin Sports Unit, located in the central area of the valley, amid a consolidated urban fabric. Given the proximity of the four buildings and their extensive complimentary program, we proposed to understand the new intervention as a single "built continent," crossed by covered streets and surrounded by squares and gardens. Rather than four independent buildings, we proposed a compact configuration, using the same structural, bioclimatic, formal, and spatial strategy.

SC. Limited times. The timeline of this project was short: two months for the competition, six months to develop the details, and a year of construction to open on the required date. To meet this difficulty, we proposed several strategies: to use metal structures, prefabricated simultaneously in four different workshops, to implement only six types of metal trusses, and to build all the stands with precast concrete pieces.

Client: Inder. Medellin Municipality
Design partner: Giancarlo Mazzanti
Opening: 2010
Program: Sports Facilities (basketball, volleyball, combat, gymnastics)
Location: Medellin
Built area: 30,000 m²
Ecosystem: Montane forest
Altitude above sea level: 1,600 m
Cost per m²: USD 1,000

EC. Parallel Stripes. The bioclimatic diagram of Medellin forces to control the morning and afternoon sun and encourages the opening of the north-south facades, faced with the predominant air currents of the valley. Therefore, we proposed a system of roofs in parallel strips that extend in the east-west direction to generate shade; they repeat in the north-south direction to gain built mass, and rise in the middle to adapt to the regulations of each sport (free heights between 12 and 16 meters).

VC. Topographic configuration. We obliged ourselves to connect the new building to the nearby hills and the mountainous topography of the city. For this reason, we avoided proposing abstract constructions and designed a topographical configuration related to the geography of the valley.

Covered public spaces. Due to the warm tropical climate of Medellin, people rarely use open public spaces during the day. For this reason, under the irregular perimeter of the roof strips, we arranged four close rectangular perimeters, generating covered streets and shady public spaces, to be used intensively by athletes and ordinary citizens. When the buildings were under construction, our client requested to incorporate a fifth handball building, which we articulated following the same rules: we repeated and expanded new roofs to cover a new rectangular perimeter.

EC. Stands. In Medellin, buildings for a big audience require an accurate architectural design to have a comfortable climate performance. In this case, we decided to build stands only on the east-west faces, so as not to block the passage of the predominant north-south air currents. We also designed perforated metal facades to allow the passage of the wind, reducing its speed. By doing this, visitors can also observe sports activities without entering the buildings.

SC. Direct contact. Local council representatives requested buildings close to inhabitants and with the same access level as the public space. For this reason, athletes access through independent ramps to the play and training areas, located 2.5 meters below the exterior level, a depth defined by a superficial groundwater level. Visitors access the corridors and service areas horizontally, and then go up to the stands to observe sports activities, keeping relation with the outside life.

SC. No Ceiling. Budget cuts did not allow the construction of a metal ceiling we designed inside all the roof strips. This situation forced us to accept an industrial appearance that reveals the operation of the building in a simple way.

SC. Tripodes. The upper trusses' structural forces and the big concrete foundations led us to design tripod-shaped columns. Two metal elements, one vertical and the other at an angle perpendicular to the facade withstand the horizontal forces of the trusses. A third element also at an angle but parallel to the facade, stiffens the structure in the longitudinal direction, carrying the drain pipes without touching the foundations.

VC. Green. For the color choice and the design of the perforations of the facades, we worked in partnership with our friend and graphic designer Juan David Diez, who chose the green tones of the roof membranes, the concrete floor, and the metal facades. He created the facade design taking photographs of small leaves that had fallen to the ground, which he organized in patterns to control the amount of airflow.

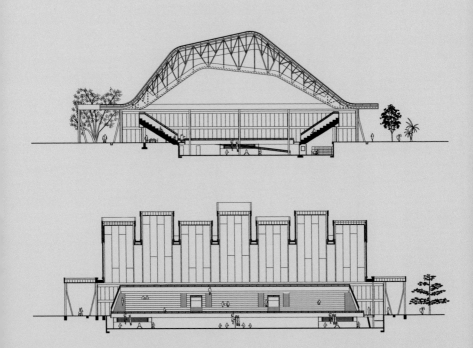

CONSTRAINTS NETWORK

EC. Avoiding the trees. The competition brief requested not to have to transplant the existing trees and to fit the new building in an irregular void inside the native forest. In previous visits to the botanical garden, we observed the existence of honeycombs and their hexagonal geometry that advances in various directions in a regular pattern. We decided to use that geometric strategy, adaptable to the irregularities of the internal outline of the forest.

SC. Uncertain budget. The client requested a project that could adapt to an unknown budget, and that could grow over time. Therefore, we proposed a building made up of modules (seven hexagons of the same size, adding to a module of 380 m^2), which we could group into different sizes and shapes. In the competition phase, we proposed fifteen modules, and finally, we built ten. We designed a building in which the modular repetition was decisive, but not the total quantity.

Client: Medellin Botanical Garden
Design partner(s): Alejandro Bernal, J. Paul Restrepo, Camilo Restrepo
Opening: 2006
Program: Facilities to expose tropical gardens - multiple spaces for events
Location: Medellin
Built area: 5,000 m^2
Ecosystem: Montane forest
Altitude above sea level: 1,600 m
Cost per m^2: USD 600

EC. Coexistence. The Botanical Garden representatives requested an ambiguous program that allowed the coexistence of tropical gardens with varied activities that will bring economic resources to the botanical garden: weddings, concerts, conferences, gastronomic and educational events, etc. Therefore, we did not propose a building with long spans and perimeter supports, but a large roof supported by groups of hollow columns that allowed the growth of gardens inside. Events and gardens coexist and mix with the structure of the building, setting up a hypo-style hall, similar to that of some mosques (for example, the Cordoba Mosque), with its deep perspectives.

EC. Trees scale. In plan, we expanded the size of the geometry of the honeycombs. In section, we directly transferred the scale of the sur-rounding trees to the project: 14 meters high between the floor and the wooden ceiling, and 2 meters thick for the cantilevered metal struc-ture, the opaque and translucent roof, and the internal wood cladding that together generated filtered light entrance.

VC. Inside out. We understood each module of seven hexagons as a pattern with technical, material, and bioclimatic qualities: geometry, the position of the gardens, rain access, collection of water, natural light entrance, temperature control, and artificial lighting system. We designed the project from inside out. From the module to the general planning, reinforcing by repetition the qualities of the building.

SC. Compact networks. The engineers requested to concentrate the hydraulic (rain and irrigation) and electrical networks in the center of each module, using the six-column metal structure as a support. We placed the artificial lights and the plant irrigation system in a ring around the columns, 6 meters high. We defined two gutter circuits on the roof, connected to exposed vertical pipes and lower water storage tanks. We designed a second metal structure to receive the wooden cladding, connecting the metal ring with the lower surface of the roof. In this way, we shaped a "vortex" that emphasizes the convergence of networks and gardens. We generated that geometry, employing hyperbolic paraboloids and forming curved surfaces from the use of straight wooden slats.

EC. Soil and winds. Architecturally, we conceived the modules to perform independently, but in reality, the whole project works in a unitary manner. Three pilotis embedded 15 meters in a low resistance floor connect to a concrete ring under each group of columns. These "hollow trunks" support the cantilevered metal roofs, which are structurally connected to form a large roof, resistant to intense horizontal wind loads.

VC. No facade. The tropical climate and the specific program allowed us to propose a building open to the surrounding forest, with a slight vertical control perimeter and an intermediate space that is never wholly an interior. We controlled the access using low pivoting doors and perimeter slopes, and hailstones with textiles located in the upper part of the hollow centers. The horizontal rains enter the building slightly, and we filtered the afternoon sun through vertical textiles that avoid the weakening of the orchids.

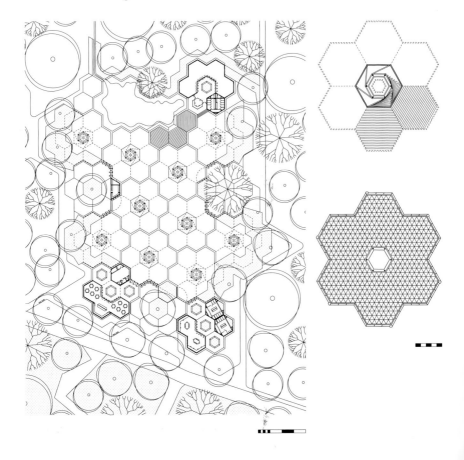

SC. Brown, green and black. Following the recommendations of our client, we proposed low-maintenance materials of rapid construction: light metal structures, cladding in pinewood grown near the city (natural brown color), floors in permeable triangular pavers, and roofs in opaque green metal tiles and translucent polycarbonate tiles. Our client widely debated all the materials, and never accepted them immediately: even the black color of the structure was discussed and chosen due to cost and a "neutral" appearance.

VC. Service buildings. During an advanced phase of the design process, our client requested three service buildings to support the main program: cafeteria, classrooms, bathrooms, and new offices for the botanical garden. They suggested the possibility that these new constructions were articulated to the geometric strategy already proposed. In this way, we designed three new modules with seven hexagons, located at the perimeter ends of the already designed structure, conceived as low buildings around patios.

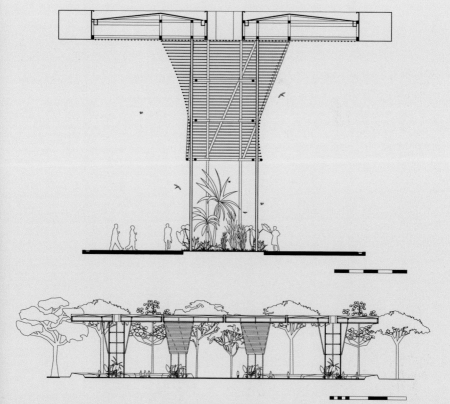

EPILOGUE

With this final text, we intend to leave the arguments of this book open, presenting another case of restricted creation, critically connected with contemporary architecture.

The Berlin-based music collective *Einstürzende Neubauten* (1980) attempted to break free from traditional western music (classical and popular) with its connections to the social and political phenomena (fascism, racism, nationalism, militarism) that led to the Second World War and the Jewish Holocaust. This group of sound artists (current members: Blixa Bargeld, N.U. Unruh, Alexander Hacke, Jochen Arbeit, Rudi Moser. Previous members: Gudrun Gut, Beate Bartel, FM Einheit, Mark Chung, Roland Wolf) connected with the experiments of some artists that expanded the possibilities of sound art during the 20th century: Luigi Russolo ("The Art of Noises" manifesto, and his *Noise Music Concerts*), Pierre Schaeffer (experiments with found and prepared objects) and John Cage (the idea of music as "organization of sound"), to name a few[1]. After the construction of the wall in 1961, West Berlin (Einstürzende Neubauten's city) was consolidated as a territory under constant development, not only due to the destructive effects of the War but also because a large number of the city's public, civic and cultural buildings, were on the east side. This phenomenon, which made evident the strong drive of a capitalist economy that quickly erased traces and marks of the city's past, strengthened in the band a critical position that led them to make creative decisions that we understand as voluntary constraints: a mix of few conventional instruments (piano, bass, guitar), lo-fi electronics, and self-made instruments using industrial debris (plates, springs, glasses, rocks, cables, etc.) to create various percussive layers; use of construction and demolition tools (drills, welders, hammers, concrete mixers, etc.) with new timbres, favoring imperfection, error, and improvisation; use of environmental sounds (cars, buildings, water tower, machines); voice and lyric experimentation (screams, whispers, silence, cries, gestures, un-text vocalization, etc.); use of unconventional sites (non-studio / concert hall venues) with raw performance, involving the audience; exploration of musical structures far from the traditional scale, and sonorous configurations distant from the conventional structure of the popular song (intro-verse-chorus-verse-chorus-bridge-chorus-outro).

This band, still active, has an ambiguous relationship with architecture. Its name, *Einstürzende Neubauten* ("Collapsing New Buildings"), implies a critical vision of the capitalist reconstruction of Berlin and its costly, transparent, and neutral buildings. Its riskiest sounds come from worn materials and construction tools. His four compilation albums (1981-2010), entitled *Strategien Gegen Architekturen* ("Strategies Against Architecture"), not only refer to the extraction of sounds through the intervention on some buildings but a vision of architecture as a discipline closely linked to power groups, too abstract, harmonious and imposed. Using their constraints, this group shakes conventional music frontally and architecture tangentially.

PLAN: B'S POTENTIAL ARCHITECTURE
Emilio Tuñón

Plan: b does architecture based on the acceptance of constraints derived from social and environmental problems and those established by the professional practice itself. For them, the ability to do architecture is no longer put in a set of unchangeable rules and knowledge but resides in a sensitivity open to the world; to this sphere, that is the heritage of people, animals, and the things that inhabit it. In this way, Plan: b's architecture builds an open work, based on a way of thinking that opens its pores to learn from what surrounds them, and is immersed in this world of constant transformation. The practice they carry out aims to widen the playing field through the critical incorporation of concepts (partial agreements, awaiting architecture, permeability, architecture in reverse, constraints) and thoughts that enrich their wonder through the endless trial of ideas and forms — which is the basis of their work. Plan: b's architecture emerges from a trial and error procedure, capable of becoming a reflection strongly anchored in the person. It is an architecture supported by a provisional humanism that arises from the acceptance that particular circumstances are drawn as a starting point. To them, theory and practice are not dissociated since the work of creating architecture goes through the continuous redefining of changing reality, restrictions, and contradictions. Only those who understand constraints as a creative opportunity can continue to consider this profession seriously. Plan: b aligns with what we like to call potential architecture, in which limitations paradoxically increase the degree of freedom by accidentally confronting and matching private obsessions with public needs.

We know of numerous examples that are pointed out and studied. We analyze the reasons why projects end up being as they are. The reason behind this is that we end up calling the causes conditions. Taxonomies have been classified according to the origin, or the intentionality of the constraints. They are opposed to the concepts; we have compared them to algorithms. They are classified as crutches, rules, obstructions, or regulations. But it is not so clear why they work, how they transform project decisions. We do not know if there is a minimum number or not. Above all we have not looked at their folds — behind them — to see what there is.

Projects are not the result of freedom but of memory. The action is to remember, to recall. Repetitions, data, experiences, examples, basis, perceptions ... Memory is a collection of diverse information. They are focal points. Ariadne's threads that allow us to get out of the labyrinth of time and appear in projects as apparitions is product of our free will. The imposition of limitations is the instrument required to order the creative paths through the Palace of Memory, transformed into critical reasons for the project. Constraints are links between the materials that define a project. Patterns above intuition, a preliminary map. The labyrinth's trap, the Palace, is dismantled.

Autonomy has no degree of movement, and there is no minimum number of constraints. Constrictions function as recognized proto-memories, or paths that we anticipate to go through, with which we go further. Although memory is unlimited, the total number of memories are fewer but still a very high number. The diagram can only be handled in that field, a set of related constraints under the appearance of a drawing. The data within is a degree of movement. A connection is a limitation, a degree of precision. To reduce a point is to focus.

When they speak to us of these self-imposed limitations, we must go back to the memory, the experience, or the repetition behind it. The hidden memory that is supporting it. The important thing is not what it becomes, but where it comes from. In this way, it reveals its value, why it has been selected. A factor or rule may not directly coincide with the architectural parameter that is apparently similar. We sometimes use a game, and it is actually the market we are talking about. Of construction, and it is repetition. Or of geometries and volumes when it is the pattern within the memory. We never reach both limits, neither to control them nor to forget them all.

NOR TO FORGET THEM ALL
Federico Soriano

NOTES

INTRODUCTION

1. Federico Mesa and Felipe Mesa. *Permeability*. Medellin: Mesa Editores, 2013. pp. 7-17. We explored the concept of "permeability" here, through seven angles, seven phenomena, and seven projects in the tropics.
2. "Constraint". Merriam-Webster Dictionary, accessed May 19, 2020, https://www.merriam-webster.com/dictionary/constraint.
3. Felipe Mesa and Alejandro Bernal *Acuerdos Parciales*. Medellin: Mesa editors, 2005. pp. 2-20. In our 2005 book Partial Agreements we explored this concept through a group of built and unbuilt projects.

ANGLES
Three questions, three types of contraints, obstacles, rules, three methods, one concept, seven crutches, one direction, five obstructions, one vow of chastity, specific problems, seven figures.

1. Michael Baxandall. Patterns of Intentions. On the Historical Explanation of Pictures (New Haven and London: Yale University Press, 1985) pp. 12-40.
2. Jon Elster. Ulisses Unbound. Cambridge: Cambridge University Press, 2000. pp. 190-221.
3. Enrique Walker. "Scaffoldings" in Luis M. Mansilla + Emilio Tuñón - From Rules to Constraints, ed. Giancarlo Valle (Zurich: Lars Muller Publishers, 2012). pp. 74-79.
4. Stan Allen, Four Projects, (San Francisco: Applied Research and Design Publishing, 2017). pp. 60-67.
5. Philip Terry (Editor), The Penguin Book of Oulipo: Queneau, Perec, Calvino, and the Adventure of Form (UK: Penguin Random House, 2019), 1-30.
6. Carles Muro, "Hacia una arquitectura potencial", Circo, 2002. pp. 97.
7. Philip Johnson, "The Seven Crutches of Modern Architecture", Perspecta vol 3 (1955). pp. 40-45.
8. David Byrne. How Music Works (Edinburgh-London: Canongate, 2012). pp. 11-18.
9. Felipe Mesa and Federico Mesa, Architecture in Reverse (Medellin: Mesaestandar, 2017). pp. 12-16. We explored this invested direction in our book "Architecture in Reverse", in which we pitted seven public educational projects against seven private residential projects. On that occasion, we reviewed the underlying contradictions that shaped them.
10. Lars von Trier and Jorgen Leth, The Five Obstructions (2003; New York, NY: Kino Lorber, 2014), DVD.
11. Rebecca Ver Straten-McSparran, "The Five Obstructions" Image Journal, Issue 93, accessed May 20, 2020, https://imagejournal.org/article/the-five-obstructions/. (I) Remake the film in Cuba, with no set, and with no shot lasting longer than twelve frames, answering the questions posed in the original movie. (II) Remake the film in a difficult place without showing that place on the screen (Leth playing the role of "the man," including the meal). He remakes the film in the red-light district of Mumbai, partially hiding it behind a translucent screen. (III) Leth Failed to complete the second task correctly, so von Trier punishes him with new obstructions: remake the film as he wants or repeats it with following the second obstruction in Mumbai again. Leth Chooses the first

option remaking the film in Brussels, using split-screen effects. (IV) Remake the movie as a cartoon. (V) von Trier has already made the fifth version, but Leth has to assume the authorship, reading a voice-over narration, written by von Trier.

12. Jorgen Leth, The Perfect Human (1968; Denmark: Laterna Film). "The Perfect Human" is a 1967 thirteen minutes short film directed by the Danish filmmaker Jorgen Leth. In it, he presents a middle-class danish couple doing daily activities in a white, abstract, and unbound room: they smoke, walk, go to bed, have dinner, etc. Here, the perfect human is a white European person, lacking a precise context. This black and white short film, with a voice-over and instrumental music in the background, is clean, refined, and controlled.

13. "Dogma 95," Dogma95.dk, Google, accessed May 21, 2020, http://www.dogme95.dk. These are the ten rules of "The Vow of Chastity":

-Shooting must be done on location. Props and sets must not be brought in (if a particular prop is necessary for the story, a location must be chosen where this prop is to be found).

-The sound must never be produced apart from the images or vice versa. (Music must not be used unless it occurs where the scene is being shot.)

-The camera must be hand-held. Any movement or immobility attainable in hand is permitted.

-The film must be in color. Special lighting is not acceptable. (If there is too little light for exposure, the scene must be cut, or a single lamp be attached to the camera.)

-Optical work and filters are forbidden.

-The film must not contain superficial action. (Murders, weapons, etc. must not occur.)

-Temporal and geographical alienation are forbidden. (That is to say that the film takes place here and now.)

-Genre movies are not acceptable.

-The film format must be Academy 35mm.

-The director must not be credited.

The rules end with a very strict commitment paragraph: "Furthermore, I swear as a director to refrain from personal taste! I am no longer an artist. I swear to refrain from creating a "work," as I regard the instant as more important than the whole. My supreme goal is to force the truth out of my characters and settings. I swear to do so by all the means available and at the cost of any good taste and any aesthetic considerations. Thus, I make my VOW OF CHASTITY."

14. Thomas Vinterberg, The Celebration (1998; Canada: Alliance Atlantis, 2004), DVD.

15. Lars von Trier, The Idiots (1998; Denmark: Tartan video, 2004), DVD.

16. Bob Gill, Forget all the rules you ever learned about graphic design. Including the ones in this book (New York: Watson-Guptill Publications/Billboard Publications, 1981), pp. 6-12.

17. Joost Elffers and Michael Schuyt, Tangram, The Ancient Chinese Puzzle (Koln: Evergreen/Taschen, 1999). pp. 7-31.

EPILOGUE

1. Jennyfer Shryane, Blixa Bargeld and Einstürzende Neubauten: German Experimental Music. 'Evading do-re-mi' (New York: Routledge, 2016), pp. 30-70.

BIBLIOGRAPHY

Allen, Stan. Four Projects. San Francisco: Applied Research and Design Publishing, 2017.

Baxandall, Michael. Patterns of Intentions. On the Historical Explanation of Pictures. New Haven and London: Yale University Press, 1985.

Byrne, David. How Music Works. Edinburgh-London: Canongate, 2012.

Elffers, Joost, and Michael Schuyt, Tangram, The Ancient Chinese Puzzle. Koln: Evergreen/Taschen, 1999.

Elster, Jon. Ulisses Unbound. Cambridge: Cambridge University Press, 2000.

Gill, Bob. Forget all the rules you ever learned about graphic design. Including the ones in this book. New York: Watson-Guptill Publications/Billboard Publications, 1981.

Google. "Dogma 95," Dogma95.dk, accessed May 21, 2020. http://www.dogme95.dk.

Johnson, Philip. "The Seven Crutches of Modern Architecture." Perspecta vol.3 (1955): pp. 40-45.

Leth, Jorgen, director. The Perfect Human. Laterna Film, 1968.

Merriam-Webster. "Constraint" (meaning b), accessed May 19, 2020. https://www.merriam-webster.com/dictionary/constraint.

Mesa, Felipe, and Alejandro Bernal. Acuerdos Parciales. Medellin: Mesa Editores, 2005.

Mesa, Felipe, and Federico Mesa. Permeability. Medellin: Mesaestandar, 2013.

Mesa, Felipe, and Federico Mesa. Architecture in Reverse. Medellin: Mesa editores, 2017.

M. Mansilla, Luis, and Emilio Tuñón. "Three Projects." In Luis M. Mansilla + Emilio Tuñón - From Rules to Constraints, Edited by Giancarlo Valle, 234. Zurich: Lars Muller Publishers, 2012.

Muro, Carles. "Hacia una arquitectura potencial". Circo, 2002, 97.

Jennyfer Shryane, Blixa Bargeld and Einstürzende Neubauten: German Experimental Music. 'Evading do-re-mi'. New York: Routledge, 2016.

Terry, Philip (Editor), The Penguin Book of Oulipo: Queneau, Perec, Calvino, and the Adventure of Form. UK: Penguin Random House, 2019.

Ver Straten-McSparran, Rebecca. "The Five Obstructions." Image Journal, Issue 93, accessed May 20, 2020. https://imagejournal.org/article/the-five-obstructions/.

Vinterberg, Thomas, director. The Celebration. Alliance Atlantis, 2004.

Von Trier, Lars, director. The Idiots. Tartan video, 2004.

Von Trier, Lars, and Jorgen Leth, directors. The Five Obstructions. Kino Lorber, 2014.

Walker, Enrique. "Scaffoldings." In Luis M. Mansilla + Emilio Tuñón - Frome Rules to Constraints, Edited by Giancarlo Valle, 74-79. Zurich: Lars Muller Publishers, 2012.

ACKNOWLEDG-MENTS

A diverse group of people was involved in various ways in the development of this book. Miguel Mesa recommended reviewing the book Patterns of Intentions written by Michael Baxandall, clarified some of the ideas presented in it, recommended reviewing the Bob Gill books, and read the manuscript several times, always making valuable suggestions. Juan David Diez commented on the concepts explored in this book, giving his perspective from graphic design (Miguel and Juan David have done the graphic design of all our books, and this case was no exception). Emilio Tuñon sent us some of his publications, recommended reviewing the work of the Oulipo Group, some texts by Carles Muro, and agreed to read the manuscript and write a paragraph about our work. Enrique Walker sent us some of his publications and agreed to read the document. Federico Soriano read the manuscript and decided to write a short text on the topics reviewed in it. Andrés Jaque had a close conversation with us about the book, his ideas and projects, and proposed to write a foreword. From Arizona State University (Herberger Institute for Design and the Arts -The Design School), Jason Schupbach, The Design School former director, always favored this project's development. Marc Neveu, architecture program Head, recommended options to publish the book and make it a reality. Claudio Vekstein made sharp and tangential comments on the topics and projects presented here. Catherine Spellman read the manuscript, helped organize the book's structure, made text corrections, and accompanied the entire process with great enthusiasm and commitment. At Applied Research + Design Publishing, Gordon Goff, founder, and Executive Publisher, was interested in the book's idea and publication, and Alejandro Guzman-Avila, Proofreader, and Project Manager collaborated by editing the text and coordinating the general development of the book. Thanks to all of them for their contributions and collaboration.

Plan: b Architects 12 Projects In 120 Constraints was finished printing
on February 2021 with Applied Research + Design Publishing, an
imprint of ORO Editions. Texts and fonts used from the Unit Pro family
were designed by Erik Spiekermann in 2003. The print run is 1,500
copies printed on 157gsm matt art paper.